In: Global Political Studies Series

BUFFER STATES

POWER POLICIES, FOREIGN POLICIES AND CONCEPTS

GLOBAL POLITICAL STUDIES SERIES

Buffer States: Power Policies, Foreign Policies and Concepts
Tornike Turmanidze
2009. ISBN 978-1-60692-901-8

In: Global Political Studies Series

BUFFER STATES

POWER POLICIES, FOREIGN POLICIES AND CONCEPTS

TORNIKE TURMANIDZE

Nova Science Publishers, Inc.
New York

For permission to use material from this book please contact us:
Telephone 631-231-7269; Fax 631-231-8175
Web Site: http://www.novapublishers.com

NOTICE TO THE READER

LIBRARY OF CONGRESS CATALOGING-IN-PUBLICATION DATA

T'urmanize, T'ornike.
[Bup'eruli saxelmcip'oebi. English]
Buffer states : power policies, foreign policies and concepts / Tornike Turmanidze.
p. cm.
Includes bibliographical references and index.
ISBN 978-1-60692-901-8 (hardcover)
1. Buffer states. 2. Georgia (Republic)--Foreign relations. I. Title.
JC323.T8713 2009
327.1--dc22
2008055354

Published by Nova Science Publishers, Inc. ✢ New York

In Memory of my Father

CONTENTS

Preface

The purpose of this book is to explore the notion of buffer states and to determine the characteristics of their foreign policy. The idea of writing such a book would less likely be born in the mind of a citizen of a big, powerful country, whereas this kind of study is in the natural scholarly interest of a person living in a small, weak state. Since it is considered that at different times Georgia played the role of a buffer state between various empires, the author decided to find out what this term means in theory and what the implications are of being a buffer state in practice, as well as which countries of the world can be identified as buffer states both at present and in the past. This study tries to answer these and other important questions.

The book consists of an introduction, seven chapters and a conclusion. The first chapter examines different understandings of the buffer state concept and suggests a new, more elaborate definition of this term. In addition, it introduces the new concept of quasi-buffer states. The second chapter focuses on the geographical and cultural characteristics of buffer states. The third chapter discusses their power criteria and makes relevant comparisons between centers of power and buffer areas in the international system. The fourth chapter depicts the geopolitical situation of buffer states and tries to apply this description to Georgia's historical and current international standing. The fifth chapter is an in-depth survey of great power rivalry over potential buffer territories in world politics. The sixth chapter focuses on the foreign policies of different buffer states. The last, seventh, chapter explains how regional buffer systems, as segments of a broader international system, operate.

ACKNOWLEDGMENTS

The major part of this book was written in 2002 in the Georgian language as part of my Master's thesis at Ivane Javakhishvili Tbilisi State University. The Georgian version of *Buffer States* was published in 2006 by a Tbilisi-based think tank BTKK – Policy Research Group as an opening volume of the series *Studies in International Politics*, introducing works by young Georgian scholars of Politics and International Relations. The idea to publish this monograph in English was generously suggested in 2007 by Nova Science Publishers, Inc., and I am very grateful to Ms. Nadya Columbus and Mr. Sergo Gotsiridze for granting me this wonderful opportunity.

I would like to thank all the people who, in a variety of ways contributed to this book. First of all, I am indebted to my colleagues Mamuka Komakhia, Revaz Bakhtadze and Gela Kvashilava for their assistance at different stages of my work. I wish to express my great appreciation to Dr. Alexander Rondeli for his encouragement and guidance of my research efforts, as well as to Dr. Zurab Davitashvili, Dr. Archil Gegeshidze and Dr. Temur Yakobashvili, who kindly reviewed my manuscript and helped me to improve it. My special thanks for valuable and congenial advices go to Erekle Urushadze and Maya Nikolaishvili.

This book would not have been possible without the tremendous support from my family: my wife Tiko Dolidze, my mother Rusudan Begishvili, my grandmother Neli Chachanidze and my late father Teimuraz Turmanidze.

Tornike Turmanidze

Tbilisi, Georgia,
September 2008

Introduction

The phenomenon of buffer states is poorly studied in the theory of international relations, even though buffers – buffer territories and buffer political units – are known to have existed since the earliest periods of human history. The word "buffer" and the phrase "buffer state" are frequently used in the vocabulary of international politics, but in most cases, the exact meaning of these terms remains unclear. Hence, I thought it would be interesting to conduct a study of the role of buffer states in the international system, especially since the buffer experience is considered historically relevant to my home country – Georgia.

To perceive a state as a buffer means to view international political processes through the prism of *realism,* the dominant theory in International Relations, as well as to accept the impact of geographical factors on international politics. Despite the numerous widely acknowledged limitations of the *realist* perspective, I consider it very viable and useful as the principles of *Realpolitik* seem to prevail even in 21st century world politics, and analyzing interstate relations in terms of power, security and struggle for influence often gives the most comprehensive answers to the questions that arise during the study of enduring rivalries and conflicts among nations in many parts of the world.

Although I do not believe that the *realist* and *geopolitical* outlooks can entirely explain the fate and the foreign policy behavior of the countries referred to as buffers, I am sure that such an approach can reveal many of their problems and help in finding solutions to them.

Therefore, in this study I shall mostly stay within the bounds of the *realist* paradigm and share its following major assumptions:

1. States are the principal actors in international relations;
2. States are unitary actors in international relations;

3. States are rational actors in international relations, which seek to maximize their power/strength;
4. States are primarily concerned with national security, which tops the hierarchy of issues in their agenda.[1]

In order to assess the role of buffer states in international politics, I think it would be essentially helpful to employ the so-called "third image" of international relations, proposed by Kenneth Waltz, the founder of the *neorealist* school of International Relations, – i.e. the international level of analysis, which considers the international system to be the chief determinant of state behavior. As Israeli scholar Michael Handel has properly put it: "Domestic determinants of foreign policy are less salient in weak states. International system leaves them less room for choice in the decision-making process."[2]

The main purpose of this book is to conduct a general theoretical analysis of the buffer state phenomenon, as well as to identify and explore important issues pertaining to it. Below, I shall successively try to:

- Define the buffer state concept (in the first chapter);
- Outline the geographical and ethno-cultural characteristics of buffer states (in the second chapter);
- Describe the geopolitical location of buffer states and answer the question whether Georgia is a buffer state (in the third chapter);
- Assess the capabilities of buffer states in the anarchical international environment (in the fourth chapter);
- Discuss the policies of great powers towards buffer states (in the fifth chapter);
- Analyze the behavior of buffer states on the international arena (in the sixth chapter); and
- Explain the logic of functioning of the buffer system, as part of the international system (in the seventh chapter).

---

[1] Paul Viotti and Mark Kauppi, *International Relations Theory. Realism, Pluralism, Globalism* (New York: Macmillan, 1987), 6, 7, 11, 32-34.

[2] Michael Handel, *Weak States in the International System* (London: Frank Cass, Second Edition, 1990), 3.

Chapter One

THE BUFFER CONCEPT

The term "buffer" was first used to denote a political unit in 1876 and the term "buffer state" – in 1883. In both cases the English spoke so of Afghanistan, which at that time was a territory separating the expanding spheres of influence of the British and Russian Empires.[3]

There are many explanations of the word "buffer" in English language dictionaries and encyclopedias. By a general definition, a buffer is:

- Something that lessens or absorbs the shock of an impact;
- One that protects by intercepting or moderating adverse pressures or influences;
- Something that separates potentially antagonistic entities, as an area between two rival powers that serves to lessen the danger of conflict;[4]
- Any of various devices or pieces of material for reducing shock or damage due to contact;
- Something that serves as a protective barrier.[5]

In addition to politics, the term "buffer" is used in the fields of technology, chemistry, computers, etc. For example, in *technology*: an apparatus for deadening

---

[3] Thomas Ross, "Buffer States: A Geographer's Perspective," in *Buffer States in World Politics,* ed. John Chay and Thomas Ross (Boulder: Westview Press, 1986), 16.

[4] "Buffer[2]," *The American Heritage Dictionary of the English Language* (Houghton Mifflin Company, Fourth Edition, 2000), http://www.bartleby.com/61/31/B0533100.html (accessed 20.01.2008).

[5] "Buffer[2]," *Merriam-Webster Online Dictionary* (Merriam-Webster, Inc., 2005), http://www.m-w.com/dictionary/buffer (accessed 20.01.2008).

impact, especially of railway vehicles;[6] in *chemistry*: a solution that can keep its relative acidity or alkalinity constant, i.e. its pH constant, despite the addition of strong acids or strong bases;[7] in *computers*: a device or area used to store data temporarily;[8] and so on.

In Georgian dictionaries and encyclopedias, the word "buffer" has a technical meaning only: a metal disc with a spring at both ends of a railroad car or a locomotive to soften collisions;[9] the function of a buffer is to withstand and reduce crash impact.[10]

The English word "buffer" is probably derived from the word "buff," which, as a *noun,* stands for a soft, thick leather made chiefly from buffalo skin and, as a *verb,* means to polish a surface with a piece of soft material. The word "buff," in turn, is either a derivative of "buffalo" (from Latin *bubalus* < Greek *βουβαλοσ*) or an imitation of making a sound like a soft body being hit. The synonyms of buffer are: barrier, shield, protection, defense, bulwark, guard, bumper, cushion, etc.[11]

In English language dictionaries, the term "buffer state" has the following meanings:

- Small state between two possible belligerents, diminishing chance of hostilities;[12]
- A neutral state lying between two rival or potentially hostile states and serving to prevent conflict between them;[13]

---

6 "Buffer," *The Concise Oxford Dictionary of Current English,* ed. J. Sykes (Oxford: Clarendon Press, Seventh Edition, 1982), 118.

7 "Buffer," *The Columbia Encyclopedia* (Sixth Edition, 2001-2005), http://www.bartleby.com/65/bu/buffer.html (accessed 20.01.2008).

8 "Buffer²," *The American Heritage Dictionary of the English Language* (Houghton Mifflin Company, Fourth Edition, 2000), http://www.bartleby.com/61/31/B0533100.html (accessed 20.01.2008).

9 "Buffer," *The Dictionary of Georgian Language,* ed. Arnold Chikobava (Tbilisi: Georgian Academy of Sciences, 1986), 65 (In Georgian language. My translation from Georgian).

10 "Buffer," *The Soviet Georgian Encyclopedia,* Vol. II (Tbilisi: Georgian Academy of Sciences, 1977), 590 (In Georgian language. My translation from Georgian).

11 "Buffer," *The Concise Oxford Dictionary of Current English,* ed. J. Sykes (Oxford: Clarendon Press, Seventh Edition, 1982), 118; "Buffer²," *The American Heritage Dictionary of the English Language* (Houghton Mifflin Company, Fourth Edition, 2000), http://www.bartleby.com/61/31/B0533100.html (accessed 20.01.2008).

12 "Buffer State," *The Concise Oxford Dictionary of Current English,* ed. J. Sykes (Oxford: Clarendon Press, Seventh Edition, 1982), 118.

13 "Buffer State," *The American Heritage Dictionary of the English Language* (Houghton Mifflin Company, Fourth Edition, 2000), http://www.bartleby.com/61/32/B0533200.html (accessed 21.01.2008).

- A usually neutral state lying between two larger potentially rival powers;[14]
- A small neutral state that lies between two potentially hostile powers and reduces the risk of conflict between them;[15]
- A nation lying between potentially hostile larger nations.[16]

As for the term "buffer zone," it is defined as follows:

- A neutral area between hostile or belligerent forces that serves to prevent conflict;[17]
- A neutral area that lies between hostile forces and reduces the risk of conflict between them. An area designed to form a barrier that prevents potential conflict or harmful contact;[18]
- A neutral zone or area between two potentially hostile nations, designed to prevent any overt acts of aggression. Any area serving to mitigate or neutralize potential conflict.[19]

It is important to mention that the term "buffer zone" has two different connotations: 1) a territory of one or more buffer states; and 2) a special demilitarized zone established by an international agreement to separate belligerents in a conflict zone. I will mostly use this term in the first sense.

The earliest attempts to explain the buffer state concept appeared in the 1930s. An American scholar Pitman Potter wrote in the *Encyclopedia of Social Sciences,* published in 1930, that "the term [buffer state] is often used to describe a weak state, small in size, probably without foreign policy of its own, which lies

[14] "Buffer State," *Merriam-Webster Online Dictionary* (Merriam-Webster, Inc., 2005), http://www.m-w.com/dictionary/buffer%20state (accessed 21.01.2008).

[15] "Buffer State," *Encarta World English Dictionary* (Microsoft Corporation, North American Edition, 2006), http://encarta.msn.com/dictionary_1861694156/buffer_state.html (accessed 21.01.2008).

[16] "Buffer State," *Random House Unabridged Dictionary* (Random House, Inc., on Infoplease, 1997), http://www.infoplease.com/ipd/A0354846.html (accessed 21.01.2008).

[17] "Buffer Zone," *The American Heritage Dictionary of the English Language* (Houghton Mifflin Company, Fourth Edition, 2000), http://www.bartelby.com/61/33/B0533300.html (accessed 21.01.2008).

[18] "Buffer Zone," *Encarta World English Dictionary* (Microsoft Corporation, North American Edition, 2006), http://encarta.msn.com/dictionary_1861694158/buffer_zone.html (accessed 21.01.2008).

[19] "Buffer Zone," *Random House Unabridged Dictionary* (Random House, Inc., on Infoplease, 1997), http://www.infoplease.com/ipd/A0354848.html (accessed 21.01.2008).

between two or more powerful states and thus serves to inhibit international aggression."[20]

In the 1940s, the buffer state phenomenon attracted the attention of Nicholas Spykman, the father of the American school of Geopolitics. According to him, buffers are "small political units located between large nations."[21]

In the late 1950s, Martin Wight, the founder of the English school of International Relations, dedicated a very interesting scholarly work to the study of buffer states – an article titled "The Pattern of Power," which was later included in his book *Power Politics*. By Wight's definition: "A buffer state is a weak power between two or more stronger ones, maintained or even created with the purpose of reducing conflict between them. A buffer zone is a region occupied by one or more weaker powers between two or more stronger powers; it is sometimes described as a 'power vacuum'."[22]

From the second half of the 20th century, buffer states have been studied in the broader context of research on small/weak states. During the last few decades, a few more detailed and comprehensive definitions of the buffer state concept were developed.

According to a Norwegian scholar Trygve Mathisen, the term "buffer" means anything like a fender or a bumper, which serves to deaden the shock or bear the brunt of collision. "A buffer state is usually defined as a small independent state lying between two larger, usually rival, states. It seems natural to think of it as a sort of political fender serving to reduce the danger of conflict between its greater neighbors. In our time [Mathisen wrote this in 1971] it seems natural to speak of buffer states not only between rival great powers, but also between rival blocs of power. The political function of buffer states between such blocs or coalitions seems to be more or less the same as that of buffers between rival great powers...".[23]

In the opinion of another Norwegian scholar Olav Knudsen: "An area may be referred to as a potential *buffer area* if it is controlled by one or more small states and located between two opposing – and much greater – powers."[24]

---

20 Pitman Potter, "Buffer State," *Encyclopedia of Social Sciences,* No. 3-4, 1930, 45.

21 Nicholas Spykman, "Frontiers, Security and International Organization," *Geographical Review,* Vol. 32, No. 3 (1942): 440.

22 Martin Wight, *Power Politics,* ed. Hedley Bull and Carsten Holbraad (London: Leicester University Press, Royal Institute of International Affairs, 1995), 160.

23 Trygve Mathisen, *The Functions of Small States in the Strategies of the Great Powers* (Oslo: Universitetsvorlaget, 1971), 107.

24 Olav Knudsen, "Eastern Europe: The Buffer Effect of a Cordon Sanitaire," in *Buffer States in World Politics,* ed. John Chay and Thomas Ross (Boulder: Westview Press, 1986), 90.

An American scholar Lawrence Ziring considers that: "Buffer states are lesser actors [in international relations] sandwiched between more powerfully endowed, ambitious, and often aggressive entities."[25]

An Israeli scholar Michael Partem refers to three elements in the buffer state concept:

1. *Geography*: the state is "lying between" two other states;
2. *Capability distribution*: the state is a "small...state...between two larger...states;"
3. *Foreign policy orientation*: the state is "independent,"[*] and its larger neighbors are "usually rival states."[26]

A Belgian scholar Stephan De Spiegeleire also highlights three elements in the definition of the term "buffer state:"

1. *Geographical element:* the buffer is located in between the buffered actors;
2. *Hierarchical element*: the buffer's power has to be significantly smaller than that of either of the buffered actors;
3. *Political element:* the buffer state has to be a truly independent sovereign[*] actor within the international system.

De Spiegeleire notes that this last political element is a necessary condition of the buffer system. When only the first two elements are present, there are two logical possibilities: 1) the state is directly dependent on one of the more powerful states and is located in its extended defense perimeter (that is when foreign troops are stationed on its territory) or 2) the state is only nominally independent and is actually divided up between the more powerful states (in this case, it lies in the sphere of influence of one or more great powers).[27]

---

25 Lawrence Ziring, "Asia's Pivotal Buffer States," in *Buffer States in World Politics,* ed. John Chay and Thomas Ross (Boulder: Westview Press, 1986), 153.

* My underlining.

26 Michael Partem, "The Buffer System in International Relations," *Journal of Conflict Resolution,* Vol. 27, No. 1 (1983): 4.

* My underlining.

27 Stephan De Spiegeleire, "Of Buffers and Bridges. Some Geodetic Thoughts on European Stability in the Post-Cold War Era," 13 January 1994, http://ourworld.compuserve.com/homepages /sdspieg/buffer.htm (accessed 24.01.2008).

A similar idea is proposed by Alexander Rondeli, the founder of the first school of International Relations in Georgia and the author of the first Georgian textbook on International Relations. In his words: "A buffer state is eventually a stable neutral zone created at the will of one or several powerful states in the space between them [...] in order to separate the opposing parties and minimize the possibility of conflict."[28]

Nicholas Spykman regards neutrality to be a necessary feature of the buffer state.[29] An American scholar John Chay holds that a small power must be neutral and independent in order to play the role of a genuine buffer in a great power rivalry.[30] Olav Knudsen also treats buffer states and satellites as different categories.[31]

Conversely, Martin Wight includes several types of countries in the buffer state concept. In his view: "Buffer states may [...] be roughly divided into trimmers, neutrals and satellites. Trimmers are states whose policy is prudently to play off their mighty neighbors against one another; the most famous of European trimmers was the Duchy of Savoy, which earned thereby first a kingdom and then the hegemony of United Italy; [...] Neutrals are states without an active foreign policy at all; their hope is to lie low and escape notice. Satellites are states whose foreign policy is controlled by another power. If the weaker state has formally conceded this control by treaty, so that in law as well as in fact it has surrendered a measure of its sovereignty, it is known as a protectorate. The gradation from trimmer to neutral, from neutral to ally, from ally to satellite, is obscure and uncertain."[32]

According to Trygve Mathisen, a buffer may be fully neutral or neutralized, as well as an ally or a controlled ally of one of its powerful neighbors.[33] For Mathisen the main element in the buffer state idea is a country's geographical location between rival great powers.

---

28 Alexander Rondeli, *The Small State in the International System* (Tbilisi: Georgian Foundation for Strategic and International Studies, Metsniereba, 2003), 160 (In Georgian language. My translation from Georgian).

29 Nicholas Spykman, "Frontiers, Security and International Organization," *Geographical Review*, Vol. 32, No. 3 (1942): 440.

30 John Chay, "Korea, a Buffer State," in *Buffer States in World Politics*, ed. John Chay and Thomas Ross (Boulder: Westview Press, 1986), 194.

31 Olav Knudsen, "Eastern Europe: The Buffer Effect of a Cordon Sanitaire," in *Buffer States in World Politics*, ed. John Chay and Thomas Ross (Boulder: Westview Press, 1986), 90.

32 Martin Wight, *Power Politics*, ed. Hedley Bull and Carsten Holbraad (London: Leicester University Press, Royal Institute of International Affairs, 1995), 160.

33 Trygve Mathisen, *The Functions of Small States in the Strategies of the Great Powers* (Oslo: Universitetsvorlaget, 1971), 109.

Thus, one may see that there is a contradiction between different definitions of the term "buffer state," suggested by several prominent scholars of International Relations. On the one hand, Spykman, Knudsen, Chay, Partem, De Spiegeleire, Rondeli and others stress that the buffer state must be truly independent and neutral and it cannot be part of some powerful country's extended defense perimeter or sphere of influence. While, on the other hand, Wight, Mathisen and others regard it as being possible for the buffer state to be a satellite of one of the great powers. Both positions have their weak points.

I presume that it is very difficult to identify buffer states by the "true independence" criterion as the latter concept is in fact obscure and there is no clear dividing line between "independence" and "dependence" or being in a "sphere of influence." Moreover, it is unrealistic to talk about the full independence and autonomy of small states in any historical period, especially if they have powerful and expansionist neighbors. Although recognized as sovereign entities by the international law, small/weak states almost never make important foreign policy decisions without taking into account the interests of great powers. Furthermore, in our time a large number of countries enjoy an unprecedented level of interdependence, which leads to a supposition that nowadays even great powers cannot be "truly independent." Yet, one must admit that there are many cases when a small state's dependence on a great power is quite evident.

Reasoning from the original meaning of the word "buffer," I hold that a neutral stance in a great power confrontation must be a necessary attribute of the buffer political unit. Thus, excluding the "true independence" aspect, I agree with the explanation of the buffer concept proposed by the first group of scholars, since the second group's position seems initially incorrect. A satellite, that is a small/weak state controlled by a great power and often occupied by it, is a phenomenon opposite to the buffer – a tool for preventing or hampering the conflict between rival great powers. A satellite may be used by one of the great powers either to attack the other or to protect itself from the possible enemy attack, but not to maintain peace.

However, despite these arguments, I do not dismiss the position of the second group of scholars as irrelevant. Some satellites really resemble buffer states and even perform the buffer function for one of the parties in conflict. For example, such one-sided buffers may be lined up with the countries called "trimmers" and "satellites" by Martin Wight or "allied buffers" and "rim buffers" by Trygve Mathisen. The latter are, in the author's words "minor powers located along the borders of great powers and coming within their defense perimeter, but [...] not situated between two great powers."[34]

I do not claim to have developed a flawless and universal explanation of the term "buffer," but I hope that my theoretical model will reconcile the two contradicting viewpoints presented above and will build a more clear and systematized definition of the buffer concept.

First of all, I consider it useful to introduce a new term "quasi-buffer" (i.e. almost buffer or half-buffer) and further to underline the difference between buffers and quasi-buffers. I will portray buffers as two-sided and multi-sided buffers and quasi-buffers as one-sided buffers. The buffer operates in two or more directions – it represents a bulwark for one as well as for the other opposing power(s), thus preventing the escalation of conflict between them. The quasi-buffer, on the contrary, operates in one direction only – it functions as a safeguard for one of the powers, thereby not helping to maintain peace between the adversaries, but rather intensifying their conflict. Hence, I put Martin Wight's trimmers and satellites, as well as Trygve Mathisen's allied buffers and, in certain cases, rim buffers into the category of quasi-buffers.

Thus, my definition of the buffer concept is closer to the one proposed by the first group of scholars, who do not recognize a weak state with a buffer geographical location as a buffer in case it is allied with one of the more powerful states. For example, Stephan De Spiegeleire writes that Cold War Eastern Europe was conceived by many as a buffer, but the appropriateness of this term had to be questioned.[35] Olav Knudsen emphasizes that members of the Warsaw Treaty Organization were not buffer states between the U.S. and the USSR.[36] Alexander Rondeli suggests that "Soviet satellites in the Cold War, the so-called People's Democracies (Poland, the German Democratic Republic, Czechoslovakia, etc) were not buffer states... some of them had Soviet troops stationed on their territories and the Soviet defense perimeter stretched along their borders. They were members of the Warsaw Pact. Therefore, it would be incorrect to call them buffers."[37]

---

[34] Trygve Mathisen, *The Functions of Small States in the Strategies of the Great Powers* (Oslo: Universitetsvorlaget, 1971), 84.

[35] Stephan De Spiegeleire, "Of Buffers and Bridges. Some Geodetic Thoughts on European Stability in the Post-Cold War Era," 13 January 1994, http://ourworld.compuserve.com/homepages/sdspieg/buffer.htm (accessed 24.01.2008).

[36] Olav Knudsen, "Eastern Europe: The Buffer Effect of a Cordon Sanitaire," in *Buffer States in World Politics,* ed. John Chay and Thomas Ross (Boulder: Westview Press, 1986), 95-108.

[37] Alexander Rondeli, *The Small State in the International System* (Tbilisi: Georgian Foundation for Strategic and International Studies, Metsniereba, 2003), 161 (In Georgian language. My translation from Georgian).

However, contrary to this opinion, I do not think that in order to be a buffer, a state has to be "truly independent" or "autonomous." A state can be turned into a buffer against its own will by two or more powerful actors – that is, neutralized – which happens very often. Many historical examples can be brought to illustrate this fact. In 1815, at the Congress of Vienna, the leading nations of Europe represented by Talleyrand, Metternich, Castlereagh and Alexander I of Russia did not ask the opinion of the Swiss whether they wished their country to be neutral; Nor in 1831 and again in 1839 did the European Great Powers (Great Britain, Prussia, Austria-Hungary, Russia and France) take into account the interests of the newly established Kingdom of Belgium. In 1831 they declared its neutrality and handed over Luxembourg, regarded by Belgium as its integral part, to the Kingdom of the Netherlands. Although the Belgian National Congress was against this decision reached at the London Conference, the Great Powers threatened Belgium with war (Prussia even moved its army towards the Belgian border). Finally, the Belgians were compelled to approve the English candidate, Leopold of Saxe-Coburg and Gotha as the first King of Belgians, instead of the French candidate, Louis Duke of Nemours, the son of the French King Louis-Philippe of Orleans, thereby endorsing the protocol of the London Conference according to which Belgium acquired a neutral [writ buffer] status. Later, in 1839 the Belgians were once again made to sign three treaties in London, signifying that Belgium finally accepted the existing state of affairs and confirmed its neutral [writ buffer] status;[38] In the 1870s and 1880s, Russia and Great Britain agreed on the buffer role for Afghanistan, ignoring the interests of its people (Afghanistan gained the right to conduct independent foreign policy only in 1919 after the Third Anglo-Afghan War), etc.

In my view, a political unit (or a group of units) of the international system, recognized as sovereign by the international law, can be considered as a buffer (buffer state or buffer zone) if the following four conditions are met:

1. *Geopolitical location.* The buffer – buffer state, buffer zone – lies in the space between rival powers of more or less the same strength (the rival powers may be represented here by states, alliances or spheres of influence. I will further call them "buffered powers").
2. *Power.* The buffer is much weaker than the two or more powers which it buffers. In case of military confrontation with either of the buffered powers, the buffer, standing alone, will be defeated.

---

38 Antoine Debidour, *The Diplomatic History of Europe,* Vol. I, (Moscow: Foreign Literature Publishers, 1947), 303-385 (In Russian language).

3. *Foreign policy orientation.* Neither of the buffered powers has its armed forces stationed on the buffer's territory. The buffer is not in a formal or informal military alliance with either of the buffered powers, i.e. it is essentially neutral to the given rivalry/conflict – either by or against its own will.
4. *Clash of security interests.* A possible military incursion by one of the buffered powers into the buffer's territory is perceived by the other buffered power(s) as a direct threat to its (their) national security.

Conversely, a political unit (or a group of units) of the international system recognized as sovereign by the international law, can be considered as a quasi-buffer (quasi-buffer state or quasi-buffer zone) if the following four conditions are met:

1. *Geopolitical location.* The quasi-buffer – quasi-buffer state, quasi-buffer zone – lies in the space between rival powers of more or less the same strength (however, in geographical terms the quasi-buffer may be closer to one of the powers).
2. *Power.* The quasi-buffer is much weaker than the single power which it buffers, as well as the latter's rival power(s). In case of military confrontation with either of them, the quasi-buffer, standing alone, will be defeated.
3. *Foreign policy orientation.* The buffered power may have its armed forces stationed on the quasi-buffer's territory. The quasi-buffer may be in a formal or informal military alliance with its buffered power against the latter's rival(s). The quasi-buffer may be part of its buffered power's defense perimeter and represent its satellite/rim guard – either by or against its own will.
4. *Clash of security interests.* The quasi-buffer acts to buffer/protect only one of the opposing powers, at the same time being a potential springboard for attack against the other power(s). The deployment of the buffered power's armed forces on the quasi-buffer's territory is a common practice, which irritates the rival power(s), but does not always cause its (their) military response. Whereas a possible military incursion by the rival power(s) into the quasi-buffer's territory is perceived by the buffered power as an attack against itself. Furthermore, over time it is possible for the quasi-buffer to change the object of buffering, which means that it can first be a shield of one power and later be used for the same purposes by another.

Thus, the buffer is essentially non-aligned and neutral, while the quasi-buffer is clearly leaning towards one side and, hence, is often viewed as a great power "property."

Chapter Two

The Geographical and Ethno-Cultural Characteristics of Buffer States

Although buffer states are generally considered to be small states, they are not necessarily small in pure geographical terms. Countries with medium or large territory and population might also become buffers (in this case they just have to be weaker than their more powerful neighbors).

An American scholar Thomas Ross assumes that the buffer potential of a territory, besides its location between two or more rival powers, is reinforced by such geographical factors as:

1. The existence of hostile physical environments on this territory (such as mountains, rugged terrain, deserts, marshlands, etc);
2. The presence of strategically important international transportation routes on this territory; and
3. The existence of zones of cultural transition or clashes between different peoples on this territory.[39]

Of course, these factors are interconnected and often simultaneously contribute to the buffer effect.

In the first case, a country develops into a buffer when the more powerful states around it do not want or do not consider its territory worth annexing due to harsh terrain or climate.[40] Historically, buffer zones were either scarcely populated or not populated at all. Hence, Nicholas Spykman has called them

---

39 Thomas Ross, "Buffer States: A Geographer's Perspective," in *Buffer States in World Politics,* ed. John Chay and Thomas Ross (Boulder: Westview Press, 1986), 14.

40 Ibid.

"waste border zones."[41] Early civilizations used marshlands, deserts, rivers, mountains, plateaus and other territories with more or less hostile terrain and/or harsh climate as buffer zones. In different historical periods, independent countries emerged on such territories and became buffer states (for example, Afghanistan, Mongolia, Nepal, Switzerland, Northern European and South Caucasian countries, etc). This kind of terrain or climate mostly served as a temporary barrier to antagonist powers and could not eventually prevent wars between them, but made the conduct of military campaigns a lot more difficult and thus helped to maintain regional peace and stability for a while.

According to Thomas Ross, of more than 200 independent states on the planet today, at least 32 have at some period during history served as buffers.[42] Interestingly, most of these countries are situated on the Eurasian continent and their territory is in fact occupied by mountains, plateaus, marshlands and other "deterrent" geographical objects.

In the second case, a country becomes a buffer when great powers are interested in the strategic transportation routes passing through its territory, but neither of the powers can claim sole control of this territory because of strong opposition from the other and, thus, both of them accept the presence of an independent state on it.[43] Historically, great powers often seemed to benefit from maintaining such territories and states as buffers (e.g. Belgium, the Netherlands, Luxembourg, Switzerland, South Caucasian countries, etc).

In the third case, a country evolves into a buffer separating or connecting two distinct cultural spheres. This phenomenon is closely related to the multicultural and multiethnic composition of population in many former or present buffer states.[44] For example, throughout history Korea was influenced by the Chinese and Japanese cultures, Uruguay – by the Portuguese and Spanish cultures, Alsace-Lorraine – by the German and French cultures, Belgium – by the Dutch and French cultures (which is exemplified by the cultural and, hence, political rift between Belgium's Flemish and Wallonian parts), and so forth. Thus, buffer states mostly possess linguistic, ethnic and religious characteristics of two or more cultures, and sometimes even civilizations, and can serve as bridges between them. For that reason, great powers have often resisted the temptation to absorb such territories fearing to have foreigners inhabit their lands. Evidently, such

---

41 Nicholas Spykman and Abbie Rollins, "Geographic Objectives in Foreign Policy, I," *The American Political Science Review,* Vol. 33, No. 3 (1939): 396.

42 Thomas Ross, "Buffer States: A Geographer's Perspective," in *Buffer States in World Politics,* ed. John Chay and Thomas Ross (Boulder: Westview Press, 1986), 20.

43 Ibid., 14.

44 Ibid.

factors as the location on strategically important crossroads, frequent conquests by powerful neighbors and ethno-cultural diversity of the society have considerably hindered many historical buffer states from developing into nation-states, thereby negatively affecting their current position on the international arena.[45]

The societies and the political elites of buffer and quasi-buffer states are often divided over their country's foreign policy orientation, which is an additional source of their weakness and yet another tool for great powers to exert influence upon them. On the example of Georgia, this has been manifested by the historical collisions of pro-Persian and pro-Byzantine, pro-Persian and pro-Ottoman and later pro-Western and pro-Russian foreign policy orientations. One interesting moment in the history of Georgia clearly illustrates this pattern. In 554, after the assassination of King Gubaz II, a people's assembly was held in the western Georgian Kingdom of Colchis (Lazica/Egrisi) to decide on which side should it continue to fight in a prolonged war between the Sassanid and Byzantine Empires. Two public speakers Aieti and Fartazi proposed almost equally reasoned foreign policy choices, the first one being pro-Persian and the other pro-Byzantine, making it very hard for the assembly to reach consensus. In the end, the decision in favor of the Byzantine Empire prevailed. A more or less similar situation has recurred many times in Georgian history; During the last few years, divisions over foreign policy orientation became evident in Ukraine as well, where the results of the 2004 presidential elections have shown that the country's northern and western regions support the idea of integration into the Euro-Atlantic structures, while its southern and eastern regions prefer a close relationship with Russia. As an influential American scholar Samuel Huntington has properly described, the territory of Ukraine is split by a fault line separating the Western and Slavic-Orthodox civilizations in Europe.[46]

---

[45] Ibid., 24.

[46] Samuel Huntington, "The Clash of Civilizations?" *Foreign Affairs,* Vol. 72, No. 3 (1993): 22-49, http://www.alamut.com/subj/economics/misc/clash.html (accessed 25.01.2008).

Chapter Three

THE GEOPOLITICAL LOCATION OF BUFFER STATES. GEORGIA – A BUFFER?

One of the major factors determining a country's buffer status is its location vis-à-vis rival centers of power in the international system. Theoretically, the spatial position of buffer and quasi-buffer states between the contending powers may take the following forms:

1. A buffer/quasi-buffer directly borders two or more rival powers – touches them by land. Examples of this include:

(In the examples listed below the distinction between buffers and quasi-buffers is temporarily omitted and a loose chronology is presented)

- The Netherlands in 1815-1831, Belgium in 1831-1945 and Luxembourg in 1867-1945, between Prussia (from 1871 Germany) and France;
- Switzerland in 1815-1945, between Prussia (Germany), France, Italy and Austria (Austria-Hungary in 1867-1918);
- Poland, Czechoslovakia and Lithuania in 1918-1939, between Germany and Russia (the Soviet Union from 1922);
- Mongolia from 1921, between China and Russia (the Soviet Union in 1922-1991);
- Afghanistan from the 1870s (as an independent state from 1919) until 1947, between Russia (the Soviet Union from 1922) and Great Britain; and in 1947-1991, between the Soviet Union and the U.S. sphere of influence (Pakistan);
- Nepal from 1947 and Bhutan from 1949, between China and India;

- Lebanon from 1948, between Israel and Syria;
- Uruguay from 1828, between Brazil and Argentina;
- Austria, Finland and Yugoslavia in 1949/1955-1991, between NATO and the Warsaw Pact;
- Angola in 1975-1990, Zimbabwe from 1965 (as an independent state from 1980), Mozambique from 1975, Botswana from 1966, Swaziland from 1968 and Namibia from 1990 until 1994 (the end of apartheid rule), between the Republic of South Africa and the countries of Sub-Saharan/Black Africa.

2. A buffer/quasi-buffer has a land border with one of the rival powers and is separated by a body of water (strait, gulf, sea, etc) from the other(s). Examples of this include:

- Korea from the Early Middle Ages until 1920, between China and from the second half of the 19th century Russia and Japan, separated from the latter by the Korea Strait; from 1945 split in two between the People's Republic of China and the Soviet Union, on the one hand, and the U.S. sphere of influence (Japan, which became an ally of the United States after the Second World War), on the other;
- Belgium in 1831-1945, between Prussia (Germany from 1871), France and Great Britain, separated from the latter by the English Channel (La Manche) and the Dover Strait (Pas de Calais);
- The Netherlands in 1815-1945, between Prussia (Germany from 1871) and Great Britain, separated from the latter by the North Sea;
- Albania in 1912-1943, between Serbia, Montenegro, Greece and Italy, separated from the latter by the Adriatic Sea and the Otranto Strait;
- Latvia and Estonia in 1918-1939, between Russia (the Soviet Union from 1922) and Germany, separated from the latter by the Baltic Sea;
- Sweden in 1949/1955-1991, between NATO and the Warsaw Pact, connected with Norway by a land border and separated from the Soviet Union and Poland by the Baltic Sea.

3. A buffer/quasi-buffer is an island located in a strategically important water system between two or more opposing powers. The examples of this include:

- Sicily, Sardinia and Corsica in the 3rd century B.C., between Rome and Carthage;
- Cuba in 1959-1991, between the United States and the Soviet Union.

A weak state between two or more rival powers may not be located at an equal distance from them. It may be often closer to one of the powers than to the other, which largely determines its geopolitical role – whether it is a buffer or a quasi-buffer. For example, as an American scholar Carlos Astiz observes, potential competitors of the United States – the dominant power in the western hemisphere – are located too far away to counterweigh its influence in Latin America.[47] Thus, when a weak state is geographically adjacent to a powerful state, it generally plays the role of its quasi-buffer. Here are some of the examples of this situation: Canada's geographical proximity to the United States resulted in it shortly becoming the latter's quasi-buffer at the onset of the Cold War; the geographical closeness of the Eastern European countries to the Soviet Union largely contributed to their joining the Communist bloc, i.e. becoming the Soviet Union's quasi-buffers; the geographical isolation from the rest of the world compelled the Kingdom of Nepal to turn into India's vassal/quasi-buffer in the 1950s, and so forth.

However, a weak state with a similar geographical location can also become a buffer or a quasi-buffer of another, distant power. This can happen when the far-away power is much stronger than the weak state's neighboring power. For instance, since 2004 some of the small countries of the post-Soviet space bordering the Russian Federation (Lithuania, Latvia and Estonia) have actually become quasi-buffers of the United States by joining the North Atlantic Alliance, instead of being buffers between Russia and NATO or quasi-buffers of Russia, while some others (Georgia and Ukraine) have been trying to acquire the same geopolitical status with different degrees of enthusiasm.

Throughout the centuries, Georgian political entities have often found themselves located in the space between much stronger powers from the south-west and the south-east, and in later centuries from the north as well:

- The Kingdoms of Iberia (Kartli) and Colchis (Egrisi) from 65 B.C. until 224 A.D., between the Roman Republic/the Roman Empire and the Parthian Empire; from the 240s until the 640s, between the Roman

---

[47] Carlos Astiz, *Latin American International Politics* (South Bend: University of Notre Dame Press, 1969), 21, quoted in: Michael Handel, *Weak States in the International System* (London: Frank Cass, Second Edition, 1990), 173.

Empire (Byzantine Empire from the late 4th century) and the Persian (Sassanid) Empire; from 650s until their final occupation by the Arabs in the 8th century, between the Byzantine Empire and the Arab (Rashidun, Umayyad) Caliphate;

- The Kingdoms of Kakheti, Hereti, Abkhazeti, Tao-Klarjeti and the Emirate of Tbilisi from the late 8th century until the mid 10th century, between the Byzantine Empire and the Arab (Abbasid) Caliphate;
- The Kingdom of Georgia from 1064 until the late 11th century, between the Great Seljuk Empire and the Byzantine Empire;
- The Kingdom of Georgia in 1256-1335, between the Il-Khanate and the Golden Horde;
- The Kingdom of Georgia in 1386-1405, between the Timurid Empire and the Golden Horde;
- The Kingdoms of Kartli, Kakheti, Samtskhe, Imereti, Guria, Samegrelo, Svaneti, Abkhazeti from the mid 15th century until losing their sovereignty in the 19th century, between the Ottoman Empire and the Persian Empire, and from 1768, the Russian Empire;
- The Democratic Republic of Georgia in 1918-1921, between Russia and Turkey;
- Georgia since 1991, between Russia and the U.S. sphere of influence (Turkey as an ally of the United States in NATO).

Since ancient times, the territory of Georgia has been an object of rivalry between various great powers *(Georgia used to be a center of power itself, perhaps, only in 1010-1964,* in 1097-1220* and in 1335-1386*)* and, therefore, for the most part it was either annexed, or incorporated into a sphere of influence, respectively by: Assyria, Urartu, Achaemenid Persia, the Seleucids, Pontus, Rome, Sassanid Persia, the Byzantine Empire, Arab Caliphates, the Seljuk Turks, the Mongol Khanates, the Ottoman Empire, Persia, Russia and the Soviet Union, as either their border province or quasi-buffer. Georgian states seldom served as genuine buffers. The true buffer states were probably only:

---

* From the creation of the unified Kingdom of Georgia until the first invasion of Georgia by the Seljuk Turks.

* From the start of the resistance against the Seljuk Turks by Georgian King David IV the Builder until the first invasion of Georgia by the Mongols.

* From the defeat of the Mongols by Georgian King Giorgi V the Brilliant until the first invasion of Georgia by Tamerlane.

- The Kingdom of Iberia (Kartli) from the 130s until 224, between the Roman Empire and the Parthian Empire;
- The Kingdom of Kakheti in 1466-1614, between the Persian Empire and the Ottoman Empire;
- The Democratic Republic of Georgia in 1918-1921, between Russia and Turkey.

From 1991 onwards, after regaining independence from the Soviet Union, Georgia has been entangled in the clash of interests between states and alliances of different power capabilities and prestige. On the one hand, Russia has been trying to hold Georgia in its sphere of influence at any cost by using a wide range of military, political and economic instruments (primarily, the conflicts in Georgia's two breakaway regions: Abkhazia and South Ossetia), while, on the other hand, the United States and its partners in NATO (which borders Georgia via Turkey) have developed active cooperation with Tbilisi since the 1990s, initially encouraged by the openly pro-Western foreign policy of Georgian President Eduard Shevardnadze (1992-2003). However, Georgia's numerous internal problems during the Shevardnadze era (losing wars in Abkhazia and South Ossetia, rampant corruption in state institutions and their inefficiency, the dictatorship of pro-Russian Aslan Abashidze in Adjara, and so on) prevented Georgia from developing consistent foreign and domestic policies directed towards integration into the Euro-Atlantic structures, thereby leaving the country's geopolitical role in the region unclear for a long time.

After the November 2003 Rose Revolution and the subsequent major successes of Georgian President Mikheil Saakashvili (regaining control over Adjara, drastically reforming state institutions, signing the May 2005 agreement with Russia, under which Moscow closed down its Soviet-time military bases in Georgia, and so on), Tbilisi's aspirations to strengthen ties with the U.S. and join NATO have become more resolute and effective, while its policy towards Russia has grown to be more staunch and sincere, thereby venturing to make Georgia's role on the Eurasian "Grand Chessboard"[48] more sharply outlined. Yet, Georgia is undergoing a period of geopolitical transition ever since 1991, because:

- On the one hand, Russia is trying to keep Georgia as its quasi-buffer, just like Belarus and other members of the CIS's Collective Security Treaty Organization (CSTO) in Central Asia: Kazakhstan and, through it, Kyrgyzstan, Uzbekistan and Tajikistan, or considers a "worse" alternative

[48] See: Zbigniew Brzezinski, *The Grand Chessboard* (New York: Basic Books, 1997).

of temporarily accepting the neutrality, i.e. buffer status of Georgia, as well as of other member states of the GUAM grouping: Ukraine, Azerbaijan and Moldova, in order to wait for a future opportunity to turn them into its quasi-buffers.

- On the other hand, Georgia wants neither to be Russia's quasi-buffer nor a buffer between Russia and the United States/NATO. Georgia's top foreign policy priority today is to leave Russia's geopolitical orbit and to fall under the Euro-Atlantic security umbrella, in fact, becoming a quasi-buffer of the United States through NATO, like the Baltic states already did in 2004. However, the extension of Russia's defense perimeter in the South Caucasus – the presence of its military bases and personnel either legally in Armenia or illegally in the Georgian provinces of Abkhazia and South Ossetia – is creating difficulties for the further expansion of the North Atlantic Alliance into the post-Soviet space and preventing Georgia from becoming either a genuine buffer or a quasi-buffer of the United States and NATO.

In the foreseeable future, Georgia as a weak, potentially buffer state, situated between the two rival centers of power may theoretically play five different geopolitical roles in the international system, which are the following:

1. *The buffer between Russia and the United States/NATO* – if Russian troops deployed in Abkhazia and South Ossetia leave Georgia, or they are replaced by an international peacekeeping contingent, while Georgia recalls its bid to join the North Atlantic Alliance and does not allow the military presence of either the U.S or any other NATO country on its soil.
2. *The quasi-buffer of the United States/NATO* – if Russian troops withdraw from Abkhazia and South Ossetia, or they are replaced by international peacekeepers, while Georgia becomes a member of the North Atlantic Alliance with a future possibility of inviting the armed forces of either the U.S. or any other NATO country on its territory.
3. *The quasi-buffer of Russia* – if Georgia agrees to keep Russian troops in Abkhazia and South Ossetia, and even allows them to be stationed on the rest of its territory with "exclusive rights," while stopping the process of integration into NATO.
4. *The shatterbelt* – if Russian troops neither withdraw from Abkhazia and South Ossetia, nor are they replaced by an international peacekeeping mission, while Georgia joins the North Atlantic Alliance with a future possibility of permitting the armed forces of the U.S. or any other NATO

country on its soil, which is, in fact, equivalent to the division of Georgia into spheres of influence by Russia, on the one hand and the United States and NATO, on the other.

5. *The economic and political bridge between Russia and the West* – if the rivalry between Russia and the United States/NATO transforms into true cooperation and friendship, Georgia maintains its territorial integrity without feeling threatened from Russia and discovers that power politics are not relevant in this region any more (the way Belgium, the Netherlands and Luxembourg left this problem behind after the Second World War as the long-lasting historical disputes between France, Germany and the United Kingdom came to an end).

The fifth scenario, which may be a continuation of the first or the second scenarios, is, of course, the best one for Georgia. However, it seems Utopian at this point, since notwithstanding Georgia's willingness and attempts to develop economic and political cooperation not only with the West, but with Russia as well, Moscow's approach to the post-Soviet space is less likely to transcend the bounds of *Realpolitik* in the near future. Therefore, Georgia is now strongly in favor of the second scenario taking into account the fact that even though Russia is weaker than the United States on a global scale, the latter is too far from the South Caucasus in order to easily balance Russia's power and influence in this region. [Sadly enough, the Russian invasion of Georgia in August 2008 might lead the country to the fourth scenario.][*]

Nevertheless, Georgia is not a buffer state today and it is hard to tell whether it will be a buffer state in the future. At least, it is evident that performing this geopolitical function is by no means Georgia's current foreign policy objective, which is very reasonable in my opinion, since being a buffer is not advantageous for a country in any way, and the following chapters will clearly demonstrate that.

---

* I added this comment during the editing of the book at the end of August 2008, amidst the ongoing Russian occupation of Georgia.

Chapter Four

THE POWER AND THE WEAKNESS OF BUFFER STATES

As already noted previously, the buffer state possesses less strength than the buffered powers. A very interesting hypothesis related to the power dimension of buffers has been proposed by Michael Partem. According to him, every buffered power considers the probability of winning a bilateral conflict with the buffer to be greater than 50%. Similarly, the buffer state thinks of its chance to withstand a bilateral conflict with any of the buffered powers to be less than 50%. Both the buffer and the buffered powers make these calculations based on their relative demographic, economic and military capabilities. Thus, Partem argues that one should not be "concerned with defining ... a small [weak] state. The buffer is simply "smaller" [weaker] than at least two of its neighbors."[49]

In order to identify potential buffer political units in the international system by the military strength criterion, Stephan De Spiegeleire suggests comparing states by their:

- Population;
- Gross domestic product;
- Defense budget;
- Armed forces;
- Main battle tanks;
- Combat aircraft

[49] Michael Partem, "The Buffer System in International Relations," *Journal of Conflict Resolution,* Vol. 27, No. 1 (1983): 7-9.

Drawing on such data, in 1994 De Spiegeleire calculated the post-Cold War military capabilities of Western Europe, Russia and their potential buffer – Central and Eastern Europe.

The first pole (Western Europe, comprising Germany, France, the United Kingdom, Italy, Belgium, the Netherlands, Luxembourg, Norway, Portugal, Spain, Greece, Turkey, Denmark, Austria, Finland, Sweden and Switzerland) had a military potential of:

- 2,694,500 serviceman
- 22,383 main battle tanks
- 6,127 combat aircraft

The second pole (Russia) had a military potential of:

- 2,030,000 serviceman
- 42,240 main battle tanks
- 4,513 combat aircraft

While the potential buffer (Central and Eastern Europe, comprising Poland, the Czech Republic, Slovakia, Hungary, Rumania, Bulgaria, Yugoslavia, Bosnia-Herzegovina, Croatia, Slovenia, Macedonia, Albania, Lithuania, Latvia, Estonia, Ukraine, Moldova and Belarus) had a military potential of:

- 1,679,487 serviceman
- 23,203 main battle tanks
- 4,233 combat aircraft

Thus, the military strength of Central and Eastern Europe, as a potential buffer, was clearly inferior to both the Western European and Russian poles.[50]

In fact, spotting buffers by their absolute and/or comparative weakness is often not so easy. After all, the power of a country cannot be measured by any mathematical formula. States certainly wage wars with the hope of winning them, but they also face the risk of improperly assessing the capabilities of their rivals. Sometimes it is impossible to determine which of the two countries is more powerful, except after they have fought a war with each other. Therefore, I hold

[50] Stephan De Spiegeleire, "Of Buffers and Bridges. Some Geodetic Thoughts on European Stability in the Post-Cold War Era," 13 January 1994, http://ourworld.compuserve.com/homepages /sdspieg/buffer.htm (accessed 15.03.2008).

that the buffer status of a state is essentially a perceptive and subjective phenomenon, determined by the personal attitude of an observer.

Nevertheless, the behavioral approaches taken by De Spigeleire, Partem and other scholars have a great practical value since differences between military potentials of many countries are quite clear. The most important moment in the power dimension of buffers, is that the buffer state cannot successfully defend its sovereignty if it stands alone against either of the buffered great powers.

Although, the comparative weakness of buffers is often fairly obvious, one can also try to discover the criteria of their absolute weakness. Buffer states are mostly *small powers*, which rank low among the actors in the international system. Moreover, states regarded as *middle powers* might be buffers as well.

Despite numerous scholarly attempts to define the term "small state/small power" based on the correlation of such tangible factors as territory, population, gross domestic product, military potential and so forth, there is no precise explanation of this concept in the International Relations literature thus far, and it is probably impossible to have one. In order to better understand the buffer state idea, I believe it would be helpful to list several definitions of both the small power and the middle power concepts.

In the words of American scholar Robert Rothstein: "...a Small Power is a state which recognizes that it cannot obtain security primarily by use of its own capabilities, and that it must rely fundamentally on the aid of other states, institutions, processes, or developments to do so." For small powers, the solution to their security dilemma must come from an outside source.[51]

A prominent American scholar, one of the authors of the complex interdependence theory, Robert Keohane groups countries into four categories according to their roles in the international system. In his opinion, "a middle power is a state whose leaders consider that it cannot act alone effectively but may be able to have a systemic impact in a small group or through an international institution; a small power is a state whose leaders consider that it can never, acting alone or in a small group, make a significant impact on the system." Thus, Robert Keohane labels middle powers as "system-affecting" states and small powers as "system-ineffectual" states, while referring to great and secondary powers [in more common terms, superpowers and great powers] as "system-determining" and "system-influencing" states.[52]

---

51 Robert Rothstein, *Alliances and Small Powers* (New York: Columbia University Press, 1968), 29, 24.

52 Robert Keohane, "Lilliputians' Dilemmas: Small States in International Politics," *International Organization,* Vol. 23, No. 2 (1969): 295, 296.

Michael Handel prefers the term "weak state," which, in his view, in addition to small powers and mini/micro states, embraces some middle powers as well. Survival is permanently on the agenda of weak states. They can hardly defend themselves not only from great powers, but sometimes from one another as well. Weak states do not weigh heavily in the international balance of power and, therefore, their defection from one side to another does not upset the equilibrium in the international system, though it can produce some minor or psychological effect. Weak states are often criticized for creating power vacuums, which invite great power aggression. The ideal type of a weak state proposed by Handel includes the following characteristics:

- Small area;
- Small population;
- In *economy*: small GNP in absolute terms; small domestic market; little or no heavy industry; high degree of specialization in a narrow range of products; high dependence on foreign capital and foreign markets for import and export;
- In *military*: inability to defend sovereignty against external threats by its own strength; high dependence on foreign military aid and weapons imports; low long-range war potential;
- In *international politics*: limited scope of foreign policy interests – only local or regional; little or no influence on the balance of power and the nature of the international system; passive foreign policy – mainly reaction to the policies of great powers; easily "penetrable;" strong appeal to the international law and international organizations; etc.[53]

Annette Baker Fox, a distinguished American expert on small states, thinks of them "as those whose leaders... recognize that their own state's political weight is limited to the local arena rather than to the global one, that they are dependent upon outside political forces for much of their security, and that their particular state's interests may be dispensable in the eyes of one or more great powers."[54]

An American scholar Amry Vandenbosch portrays weak states as *consumers* of security and attributes their minor role in international politics and their

[53] Michael Handel, *Weak States in the International System* (London: Frank Cass, Second Edition, 1990), 9-60.

[54] Annette Baker Fox, "The Small States in the International System, 1919-1969," *International Journal*, No. 24 (1969): 751. n. 3, quoted in: Michael Handel, *Weak States in the International System* (London: Frank Cass, Second Edition, 1990), 42. n. 92.

perception by great powers as potential vassals rather than equals to their military and diplomatic weakness.[55]

According to Alexander Rondeli, all scholars writing about the problems of small states emphasize the fact that "a small state is ultimately a weak state in military and political terms, which cannot defend its national interests in the international system on its own."[56]

An American scholar Herbert Goldhamer writes that "[t]he term *smaller country* seems to be reserved for large countries with small populations, small countries with small populations, and sometimes countries of any size that mostly mind their own business in world affairs."[57]

In the phrase of a Dutch scholar L. Jaquet, "a small state is a state that is neither on a world scale nor on a regional scale able to impose its political will or protect its national interests by exerting power politics."[58]

Since buffer states are categorized as small/weak states, much of what can be said about the latter holds true for buffers as well. Although, here I will only reveal the attributes of small/weak states that can either enhance or reduce their buffer potential.

The low self-defense of weak states is a significant obstacle to their formation and functioning as buffers since opposing great powers are always appalled by the existence of power vacuums between them: each of them suspects that the other is planning to occupy the buffer, establish military bases on its territory and use it as a launching pad for an attack. Hence, in order for weak states to successfully carry out the buffer function, their military forces need to be as well-trained and strong as possible. This might persuade the suspicious neighbors that the weak state in

---

55 Amry Vandenbosch, "The Small States in International Politics and Organization," *The Journal of Politics,* Vol. 26, No. 2 (1964): 294, 301.

56 Alexander Rondeli, *The Small State in the International System* (Tbilisi: Georgian Foundation for Strategic and International Studies, Metsniereba, 2003), 25, 26 (In Georgian language. My translation from Georgian).

57 Herbert Goldhamer, *The Foreign Powers in Latin America* (Princeton: Princeton University Press, 1972), 237, n. 29, quoted in: Michael Handel, *Weak States in the International System* (London: Frank Cass, Second Edition, 1990), 9; Alexander Rondeli, *The Small State in the International System* (Tbilisi: Georgian Foundation for Strategic and International Studies, Metsniereba, 2003), 25 (In Georgian language).

58 L. G. M. Jaquet. "The Role of Small States within Alliance Systems," in *Small States in International Relations,* ed. A. Schou and A. Brutland (Stockholm: Almquist and Wiksell, 1971), 58, quoted in: Michael Handel, *Weak States in the International System* (London: Frank Cass, Second Edition, 1990), 61; Alexander Rondeli, *The Small State in the International System* (Tbilisi: Georgian Foundation for Strategic and International Studies, Metsniereba, 2003), 25 (In Georgian language).

question can defend its neutrality and buffer status from minor threats as a minimum.

The policy of armed neutrality is a very heavy burden for weak states, the majority of which cannot afford to produce or buy modern weapons and maintain large armies due to their limited economic potential. The inevitability of being defeated in a war with a great power often results in *defense nihilism* on the part of weak states, that is in their total refusal to build armed forces. This occurs when the government of a weak state believes that no matter what it does to strengthen its military potential, it cannot repel an attack of a great power, therefore it considers defense expenditures to be a waste of resources. However, it is also true that a strongly resisting army, even if small, can greatly contribute to halting aggression. A weak state can deter a more powerful state from attacking it if it clearly demonstrates that prior to achieving victory a potential aggressor will lose a large amount of its troops, military equipment, time and will have to maintain a large portion of its military forces on the occupied territory, i.e. its strategic accomplishments will be outweighed by tremendous costs. As a hypothetical example, "[in 1914] Holland's ability to mobilize an army of up to 450,000 soldiers may have helped it maintain its neutrality during the First World War,"[59] or, similarly, "Belgium and Holland effectively armed *might* have had a considerable impact on the way in which both World Wars were fought."[60]

A potential buffer state, which portrays itself as an unattractive target, can really become a successful buffer. At least, the probability of its survival and its ability to prevent military hostilities between the buffered powers will increase. As Michael Handel assumes, the longer a weak state can resist an attack by a great power, the higher are its chances to receive help from another great power.[61]

However, if the rival great powers nonetheless choose to start a war, the buffer will not be able to stop them, its territory will be turned into a battlefield and after the end of the war its fate will be decided by the winner. This has happened many times throughout history to Poland, Belgium, Afghanistan, Georgia and other countries.

The vulnerability of weak states is further increased by such geographical factors as small territory, flat terrain, good climate conditions, small and sparse population, etc. If a country is small in size, its army has no *strategic depth,* i.e. not much territory to withdraw and, hence, the loss of the first battle for such a

---

59 Michael Handel, *Weak States in the International System* (London: Frank Cass, Second Edition, 1990), 76-104, 102.

60 Robert Rothstein, *Alliances and Small Powers* (New York: Columbia University Press, 1968), 172.

61 Michael Handel, *Weak States in the International System* (London: Frank Cass, Second Edition, 1990), 92.

country can often mean its final defeat in a war. The absence of natural strategic barriers (such as mountains, for instance) also limits the maneuverability of a weak state's armed forces, while small population or sparsely populated territory results in it having a small and ineffective army. Conversely, if a country has a somewhat large territory, difficult terrain and bad climate conditions (like Afghanistan, Switzerland, Finland and others), its defense capabilities are relatively strong and a hostile nation will not easily set its mind on waging war against it.[62] Therefore, such a state can be a better buffer.

Stephan De Spiegeleire maintains that the buffer effect – the buffer's ability to prevent armed conflict between the rival great powers – in addition to certain geographical factors (e.g. large territory and natural geographical obstacles) is enhanced by such economic and political factors as a viable national economy, lack of strategic resources coveted by any of the buffered powers, domestic political cohesiveness and stability. Moreover, in order for the buffer state to survive, the buffered actors must not be encouraged to intervene in its domestic affairs.[63]

A weak state's vulnerability and unstable buffer status is often reinforced by the fact that its territory bears enormous strategic importance for at least one of the contending great powers. In this case, the more interested strong party will try hard to conquer its weak neighbor and force it into an alliance, regardless of the level of its resistance. For example, in 1939, the Soviet Union started the Winter War in order to occupy the territory of Finland, which it feared might have become a springboard for German aggression (the southern border of Finland was only 32 kilometers away from the city of Leningrad).[64] Quite often the plight of buffer states is aggravated by the border disputes initiated by their powerful neighbors.[65]

In the opinion of Olav Knudsen, the buffer effect can be positively influenced by the buffer state's commitment to continued independence and desire for freedom from great power influence, evidenced in its domestic and foreign policy acts.[66] Buffer states are often capable of effectively defending their sovereignty

---

[62] Ibid., 67-90.

[63] Stephan De Spiegeleire, "Of Buffers and Bridges. Some Geodetic Thoughts on European Stability in the Post-Cold War Era," 13 January 1994, http://ourworld.compuserve.com/homepages/sdspieg/buffer.htm (accessed 17.03.2008).

[64] Michael Handel, *Weak States in the International System* (London: Frank Cass, Second Edition, 1990), 72.

[65] Alexander Rondeli, *The Small State in the International System* (Tbilisi: Georgian Foundation for Strategic and International Studies, Metsniereba, 2003), 167 (In Georgian language).

[66] Olav Knudsen, "Eastern Europe: The Buffer Effect of a Cordon Sanitaire," in *Buffer States in World Politics,* ed. John Chay and Thomas Ross (Boulder: Westview Press, 1986), 91.

and buffer status thanks to the heroism of their armed forces and people. For example, in the 13th century the Holy Roman Empire was trying to strengthen control of the St. Gotthard Pass, which was part of an important trade route connecting the lands of Italy and Germany, but the local communities of Uri, Schwyz, and Unterwalden formed an alliance in 1291 and in 1315 defeated a much larger army of the Habsburgs at the battle of Morgarten, later establishing the Swiss Confederacy together with Lucerne, Zürich, Berne and other cities; Similarly, in the First Anglo-Afghan War of 1839-1842, the British could not crush the resistance of the Afghan people, otherwise this country would have become part of the British Empire years before Russia increased its influence in Central Asia; Also, because of the fierce fighting by the Finns against the Soviet army in 1939-1940 and again in 1944, this country was able to retain its independence and buffer status during the Cold War. In a conversation about Finland at the Tehran Conference of 1943, Stalin told Roosevelt and Churchill: "any nation that fought with such courage for its independence deserves consideration."[67]

However, effective military force alone cannot safeguard a country's buffer status. The fact that Switzerland and Sweden were left unharmed in the First and the Second World Wars, as well as the phenomenon of *Finlandization* during the Cold War, is explained by some scholars not as much by the well-developed military potential, self-sufficient arms industry or high percentage of total population serving in the military in these countries, but rather by their minor geostrategic importance at a given historical moment. Michael Handel, for example, believes that Sweden and Switzerland were saved due to their location on the periphery of confrontation – in areas not essential for direct fighting between the Entente and the Central Powers in the First World War and the Allies and the Axis Powers in the Second World War, while equally neutral and heavily armed Belgium and Poland could not withstand foreign aggression and stay out of these wars;[68] Trygve Mathisen also points to the fact that during the Second World War Switzerland was entirely surrounded by the territories controlled by Germany and its allies and, therefore, it was hard to see any reason why Hitler should have wanted to occupy this "neutral island," especially if such a step could have strained German-Italian relations. The same happened with Sweden at that

---

[67] Max Jakobson, "Finland: A Nation that Dwells Alone," *The Washington Quarterly*, Vol. 19, No. 4 (1996): 41, quoted in: Alexander Rondeli, *The Small State in the International System* (Tbilisi: Georgian Foundation for Strategic and International Studies, Metsniereba, 2003), 169 (In Georgian language).

[68] Michael Handel, *Weak States in the International System* (London: Frank Cass, Second Edition, 1990), 102.

time;[69] Later, the Soviet Union welcomed Sweden's neutrality in the Cold War as it had no common land border with this country. After the end of the Second World War, a number of factors positively influenced the fate of Finland. In the view of Alexander Rondeli, the location of this country on the northern periphery of Europe, as well as the expected troubles which might have followed a new attempt to seize its territory, most likely convinced Stalin that Finland's buffer status was acceptable to the Soviet Union.[70]

[69] Trygve Mathisen, *The Functions of Small States in the Strategies of the Great Powers* (Oslo: Universitetsvorlaget, 1971), 259.

[70] Alexander Rondeli, *The Small State in the International System* (Tbilisi: Georgian Foundation for Strategic and International Studies, Metsniereba, 2003), 169 (In Georgian language).

Chapter Five

Power Politics and Buffer States

The buffer phenomenon is probably as old as mankind. Even prehistoric tribes left certain territories between the areas of their settlement uninhabited in order to avoid regular contact and, thus, reduce the probability of brutal clashes among one another. The practice of maintaining such "no-man's lands" did not disappear after the emergence of early civilizations. Following the creation of states and their evolving into great and small powers, the rival great powers often chose either to maintain "waste border zones" or to establish weak states – buffers or quasi-buffers – in areas between them, so as not to be in direct touch with each other.

A situation when a weak area – a potential buffer zone composed of weak political units – emerges between two power poles [as, for instance, in Europe after the First and the Second World Wars and the Cold War; in the South Caucasus after the 1917 revolutions in Russia and again after the collapse of the Soviet Union; in Central Asia after 1991, etc.] can theoretically lead to one of the following two outcomes:

1. The middle area can be perceived as an unstable vacuum to be stabilized either by the unilateral extension of the defense perimeter of one of the power poles (e.g. the subjugation of the Eastern European countries by the Soviet Union after the Second World War, the expansion of NATO to the east after the Cold War, etc.) or by the partitioning of this area into spheres of influence, i.e. by the simultaneous extension of both power poles' defense perimeters, based on a "gentleman's agreement" between them (e.g. the division of Eastern Europe by Nazi Germany and the Soviet Union under the Molotov-Ribbentrop Pact of 1939, etc.).

2. The middle area can be recognized as a true stabilizing buffer zone (e.g. Eastern Europe in 1918-1939, etc).[71]

Throughout history great powers have more often opted for the first rather than the second outcome, because of being afraid of power vacuums, on the one hand, and having a huge appetite for expanding their borders and spheres of influence on the other. The earliest known peace treaty in world history, concluded in c. 1258 B.C. between the Egyptian Pharaoh Ramesses II and the Hittite King Hattusili III actually implied the splitting up of a potential buffer territory between the two empires, namely that of present-day Syria and Palestine, which included the cities: Halab, Alalakh, Kadesh, Nukhashi, Amuru, Carchemish and others. Eventually, the cities in the north were subdued by the Hittites and the cities in the middle and in the south – by the Egyptians; The Roman and Parthian Empires never used Armenia, which was located between their farthermost borders, as a genuine buffer and instead vied for control over its territory. In the 1st century B.C. Armenia became a vassal of Rome (together with Georgian Kingdoms of Iberia and Colchis and the Caucasian Kingdom of Albania), but in 66 A.D., the Roman Emperor Nero was forced to yield Armenia to Parthia;[72] Since the tripartite division of Charlemagne's Empire under the Verdun Treaty of 843, its middle territory (the one between rivers Rhein and Rhone) served as a natural barrier between the French and German states for many centuries that followed, however, both the French and German rulers persistently tried to conquer this territory, encompassing modern-day Belgium, the Netherlands, Luxembourg, Alsace-Lorraine and Switzerland;[73] Under the 1555 Amasya treaty, the Persian and Ottoman Empires partitioned the South Caucasus: western Georgia was occupied by the Ottomans, eastern Georgia by the Persians, and southern Georgia (Samtskhe), which could have been an effective buffer between these two empires, was also bifurcated; The Anglo-Russian Entente of 1907 resulted in the division of Persia into their spheres of influence: the country's northern part became the Russian zone and its southern part the British zone,

[71] Stephan De Spiegeleire, "Of Buffers and Bridges. Some Geodetic Thoughts on European Stability in the Post-Cold War Era," 13 January 1994, http://ourworld.compuserve.com/homepages/sdspieg/buffer.htm (accessed 20.03.2008); Michael Partem, "The Buffer System in International Relations," *Journal of Conflict Resolution,* Vol. 27, No. 1 (1983): 19.

[72] *The History of Diplomacy,* Vol. I, ed. Vladimir Potiomkin (Moscow: GSEI, 1941), 20-22, 77-80 (In Russian language).

[73] Samuel van Valkenburg and Carl Stotz, *Elements of Political Geography* (Englewood Cliffs: Prentice Hall, Second Edition, 1954), 41, quoted in: Thomas Ross, "Buffer States: A Geographer's Perspective," in *Buffer States in World Politics,* ed. John Chay and Thomas Ross (Boulder: Westview Press, 1986), 18.

leaving only a narrow neutral zone in between; In the same year, France and Great Britain reached a much similar agreement on Thailand, which until that time had been separating their spheres of influence in South-East Asia: the country's western part fell under British control, while its eastern part was taken by the French; After the Second World War, the United States and the Soviet Union turned down the idea of using Korea as a buffer and extended their defense perimeters on the Korean Peninsula, breaking up the country across the 38th parallel; The Great Powers of Europe seldom granted the Eastern European states enough independence to enable them to function as buffers. Poland has always been a natural separator of the Slavic and German civilizations. However, in the 18th century Prussia, Russia and Austria partitioned it three times (in 1772, 1793 and 1795), later in 1939, Nazi Germany and the Soviet Union did to it the same, and after the Second World War, the country was incorporated into the Soviet sphere of influence; By the beginning of the 1990s, Eastern Europe obviously satisfied the criteria for becoming a buffer, as an area of independent states interposed between, and inferior in terms of power to, the Western and Russian poles.[74] But the United States and its Western European allies refused to make this region a buffer and decided to fill the geopolitical power vacuum, which emerged here after the end of the Cold War, by expanding the North Atlantic Alliance to the east, thus meeting the will of the majority of Eastern European nations (including the Baltic states), whose "historical memories keep the buffer function as a symbol of painful and tragic experience."[75]

Great powers are generally tempted to invade the potential buffer area and to infringe upon the existing buffer due to the lack of trust towards each other – in other words, because each of them is afraid that the other might wield influence over the buffer, turn it into its quasi-buffer and then use it as a springboard for further expansion. For example, from the end of the 19th century, the Japanese repeatedly claimed that Korea was too weak to maintain independence and therefore they had to absorb it;[76] In 1970, U.S President Richard Nixon justified the invasion of Cambodia [then a buffer state] by the fact that the North Vietnamese had planned to occupy Laos and Cambodia in order to outflank and

---

[74] Stephan De Spiegeleire, "Of Buffers and Bridges. Some Geodetic Thoughts on European Stability in the Post-Cold War Era," 13 January 1994, http://ourworld.compuserve.com/homepages /sdspieg/buffer.htm (accessed 25.03.2008).

[75] Alexander Rondeli, *The Small State in the International System* (Tbilisi: Georgian Foundation for Strategic and International Studies, Metsniereba, 2003), 164 (In Georgian language. My translation from Georgian).

[76] John Chay, "Korea, a Buffer State," in *Buffer States in World Politics,* ed. John Chay and Thomas Ross (Boulder: Westview Press, 1986), 195.

attack American forces in South Vietnam. Furthermore, Henry Kissinger, the National Security Advisor to the President, said: "[W]e are not interested in Cambodia. We're only interested in it not being used as a base;"[77] The same kind of fear provoked the occupation of Lebanon by Syria in 1976 and the subsequent invasion of southern Lebanon by Israel in 1982. Such a threat materialized again in the summer of 2006, when Hezbollah bombed Israeli military positions from Lebanese territory, entailing another full-scale military campaign by Israel in southern Lebanon; The German ultimatum to Belgium of 2 August 1914, requesting free passage of its army through Belgium towards France, was perceived as a national security threat not only by France, but by Great Britain as well. On 3 August, British Foreign Secretary Sir Edward Grey argued before the Parliament that Great Britain would have to fight a war if Belgium's neutrality was violated by foreign military aggression. Consequently, on 4 August, Britain entered the First World War."[78]

Thus, great powers are concerned with the threats emanating from their weak neighbors, which are sometimes imaginary and sometimes real. For instance, the Japanese and the Chinese used metaphors describing Korea, respectively as a "dagger" pointed at the heart of Japan and a "hammer" ready to strike at the head of China.[79] The fact that a buffer state can let its territory be used as a military corridor by one of the great powers (either at its own will or as a result of coercion) makes it really dangerous for another great power to acquiesce to the existence of a weak, neutral state at its borders. That is why, whenever possible, great powers refuse to preserve neutral buffers between one another and try to gain influence over their smaller neighbors. As Trygve Mathisen observes: "Stronger powers have often endeavored to include minor powers along their borders into their defense system. The idea is to be able to take up defense at the borders of these minor states, and in this way extend the depth of defense. Even the Soviet Government has advocated this view, and maintained that the Red Army ought to be able to take up defense at the borders of the smaller neighbors of the Soviet Union, despite the fact that this enormous power has a greater depth of defense than any other single state [as of 1971]. The advantage of this strategy is obvious. It not only increases the chances of repelling an aggressor, but if

[77] Henry Kissinger, *White House Years,* Vol. I (Boston: Little, Brown, 1979), quoted in: Michael Partem, "The Buffer System in International Relations," *Journal of Conflict Resolution,* Vol. 27, No. 1 (1983): 10-11.

[78] *The History of Diplomacy,* Vol. I, ed. Vladimir Potiomkin (Moscow: GSEI, 1941), 265 (In Russian language).

[79] John Chay, "Korea, a Buffer State," in *Buffer States in World Politics,* ed. John Chay and Thomas Ross (Boulder: Westview Press, 1986), 192.

defense is successful from the beginning, only these rimstates will become the battleground, and the territory of the major power may be largely spared the devastations of war. This category of powers is often called "buffer states.""[80]

According to the research conducted by an American scholar, Tanisha Fazal, on the question of the survival of states in the international system, buffer states are more likely to die than nonbuffer states, and unallied buffer states are more likely to lose their sovereignty and disappear than buffer states allied with a great power.[81]

Powerful states often assign their weak neighbors the function of a barrier blocking the expansion of their rivals and/or of a bridge-head for military offensives against their enemies. Great powers with access to the sea seek to establish buffer states on opposite shores from their own to have a stronghold or a stepping-stone for further actions on these coasts. For example, Britain traditionally used Portugal and Belgium for restraining, respectively, Spanish and Franco-German aggression and conducting military operations on the Continent. The Anglo-Portuguese friendship has been called "the oldest of the European alliances" – the independence of Portugal guaranteed the safety of Britain's sea routes in the Atlantic. Another goal of the British foreign policy on the mainland has long been to prevent France from absorbing the territory of Belgium. Among the several causes of the Anglo-French Hundred Years' War (1337-1453) were France's recurring attempts to invade Flanders. In the second half of the 17th century, Louis XIV of France waged three wars to conquer the Low Countries, namely in 1667-1668, 1672-1678 and 1688-1697, but each time confronted the coalitions led or joined by Great Britain. According to the "Grand Design" attributed to Henry IV of France (the grandfather of Louis XIV), France was to be surrounded by weak states under its protection; By the same logic, in the 530s, the Byzantine Empire built large fortifications in the western Georgian Kingdom of Colchis (Lazika/Egrisi) in an effort to hold back the expansion of Sassanid Persia towards the Black Sea; In the beginning of the 13th century, the Kingdom of Georgia, being at the peak of its power under Queen Tamar, maintained a belt of buffer and quasi-buffer territories along its borders: Ossetia (Alania), Dzurdzuketi (today's Chechnya and Ingushetia), Didoeti (today's western Dagestan), Khundzag (Avar Khanate), Leketi (today's eastern Dagestan) to the north, Shirvan, Adarbadagan, Arran, Nakhchivan to the south-east, Erzincan, Erzurum and the Empire of Trebizond to the south-west, – all for the purpose of keeping

---

[80] Trygve Mathisen, *The Functions of Small States in the Strategies of the Great Powers* (Oslo: Universitetsvorlaget, 1971), 84-85.

the strategic distance from its Muslim rivals, which were: the Seljuk Sultanate of Rum, the Artuqids, the Ayyubids, the Zengids of Mosul and the Eldeguzids. However, in 1210, Georgia had to recognize the Ayyubid influence on Ahlat (the Shah-Armen State); In the 19th century, the British Empire maintained several satellite states along the northern border of its colony India, namely Nepal, Bhutan and Sikkim; After annexing Korea in 1910, Japan invaded Manchuria in 1931-1932 and established a puppet state of Manchukuo on its territory; In 1921, Russia detached Outer Mongolia from China and turned it into a buffer state, at the same time annexing its northern part Tuva; In the 1950s, the United States fortified Canada with air defense radars and other military arrangements so as to have a shield against possible Soviet attack from the north; In 1939 the Soviet Union demanded territorial concessions from Finland, justifying this move by strategic and defense needs in an expected war with Germany, which, in the case of landing troops in south Finland, could have easily occupied the city of Leningrad. Furious at the unsuccessful Winter War of 1939-1940, the Soviet Union gained momentum after the Second World War and took away Karelia from Finland, thus denying it access to the Barents Sea; From the beginning of the Cold War, the United States has supported Turkey and Pakistan as its major outposts in Eurasia. When the Soviet Union attempted to take control of the Black Sea straits in 1947, the United States responded by promulgating the Truman Doctrine, which associated Turkey's independence with U.S. national interests. In the following decades, largely owing to American military aid, Turkey grew from a quasi-buffer to a regional power – the key ally of the United States in the region. The United States also supported Pakistan throughout the Cold War in order to contain the expansion of the Soviet and Chinese spheres of influence in Asia.[82]

Thus, states try to deal with threats to their national security as far from their borders as possible. Napoleon used to repeat this old maxim of French military strategy: "If you would defend the left bank of the Rhine, cross to the right."[83] The policies of rivalling great powers towards each other, as well as towards potential buffer territories can be briefly described by this old Georgian proverb,

---

81 Tanisha Fazal, "State Death in the International System," *International Organization,* Vol. 58, No. 2 (2004): 314, 316.

82 *The History of Diplomacy,* Vol. I, ed. Vladimir Potiomkin (Moscow: GSEI, 1941), 97, 204-207, 213-215 (In Russian language); Martin Wight, *Power Politics,* ed. Hedley Bull and Carsten Holbraad (London: Leicester University Press, Royal Institute of International Affairs, 1995), 161-164; Trygve Mathisen, *The Functions of Small States in the Strategies of the Great Powers* (Oslo: Universitetsvorlaget, 1971), 62-66.

83 Martin Wight, *Power Politics,* ed. Hedley Bull and Carsten Holbraad (London: Leicester University Press, Royal Institute of International Affairs, 1995), 150.

which literally translates into English as: "Quarrel on the other bank of the river and this bank will stay yours."

Hence, great powers struggle for influence over buffer territories and are mostly interested in filling the power vacuum between them by their quasi-buffers rather than neutral buffers. As Martin Wight asserts: "Each stronger power will generally have a vital interest in preventing the other from controlling the buffer zone, and will pursue this interest in one of the two ways, according to its strength. It will seek either to maintain the buffer zone as neutral and independent, or to establish its own control, which may lead in the long run to its annexing the buffer zone and converting it into a frontier province [...] Fluctuations of power make most buffer zones unstable and ambiguous. A policy adopted by one great power to preserve the neutrality of a buffer state may be seen by its rival as reducing the buffer state to a satellite; and a buffer state may be regarded by the same statesman, in different circumstances, as either a defensive bulwark or a springboard for further expansion."[84]

Reasoning from the above, one can assume that buffer states might not emerge in a power vacuum at all, or if they do, their independence might sooner or later be challenged by the preventive military actions of their stronger neighbors. Nevertheless, buffer states have existed thus far and they are not likely to totally disappear in the near future.

By the end of the First World War, the founder of the English school of Geopolitics Sir Halford Mackinder promoted the idea of establishing a belt of buffer states between the Slavic and German civilizations in order to save the "Heartland" and the "World-Island" from falling under the control of a vast empire based on land power, which could have evolved in the result of a possible German-Russian alliance. Moreover, this had to be done to prevent the decline of sea power, epitomized, first of all, by Great Britain.[85] The idea of using Eastern Europe as a buffer separating Germany and Russia was embraced by the British and French delegates to the Paris Peace Conference. Hence, nine Eastern European states (Lithuania, Latvia, Estonia, Poland, Czechoslovakia, Hungary, Romania, Yugoslavia and Bulgaria) made up a buffer zone, the so-called "cordon sanitaire," between the defeated Germany and the resurgent Russia to halt the spread of Communism in Europe, on the one hand, and to divert Germany's attention to the east, on the other. However, the outbreak of the Second World War in 1939 proved that the Eastern European buffer did not work. It neither

---

84 Ibid., 160-161.

85 See: Halford Mackinder, *Democratic Ideals and Reality* (New York: Henry Holt and Company, 1919).

avoided war in Europe, nor did it contain the Red Danger. On the contrary, it favoured the young Communist empire to a certain extent.[86] As a famous British historian A. J. P. Taylor noted: “The cordon sanitaire worked also the other way round, though this was less perceived for some years. It excluded Russia from Europe, but it also excluded Europe from Russia. In a perverse way, the barrier designed against Russia became Russia's protection.”[87]

Despite a lot of failures in the course of history, the buffer phenomenon’s positive effect on the stability of the international system is still broadly acknowledged. For example, it is considered that during the Cold War the utility of Laos as a buffer keeping apart the Communist and Western spheres of influence in Southeast Asia was greater than that of partitioned Vietnam, where the two ideologies came into direct contact, bringing about a war.[88] A top U.S. diplomat and the mastermind of the policy of Containment, George Kennan wrote in 1956: “I think it... a good thing rather than a bad thing that Sweden has never joined the Atlantic Pact, that Switzerland has preserved in every respect her traditional neutrality, that Austria has been effectively neutralized, and that Yugoslavia is not wholly committed either to West or to East. I would wish that this neutral zone might be widened, rather than narrowed. While I realize that the concept of neutrality can be, and has been, exploited for Communist purposes, I don't think that should deter us from recognizing the real advantages it may hold.”[89]

In a *realist* world, the territorial contiguity factor raises the probability of international conflicts since each state perceives threats primarily from its immediate neighbors, which have more opportunities for attacking it. In the view of Martin Wight: “It is a general rule that when powers are territorial neighbours,

---

[86] Stephan De Spiegeleire, “Of Buffers and Bridges. Some Geodetic Thoughts on European Stability in the Post-Cold War Era,” 13 January 1994, http://ourworld.compuserve.com/home pages/sdspieg/buffer.htm (accessed 14.04.2008).

[87] A. J. P. Taylor, *The Origins of the Second World War* (New York: Althenium, 1961), 37, quoted in: Olav Knudsen, “Eastern Europe: The Buffer Effect of a Cordon Sanitaire,” in *Buffer States in World Politics,* ed. John Chay and Thomas Ross (Boulder: Westview Press, 1986), 87; Stephan De Spiegeleire, “Of Buffers and Bridges. Some Geodetic Thoughts on European Stability in the Post-Cold War Era,” 13 January 1994, http://ourworld.compuserve.com/home pages/sdspieg/buffer.htm (accessed 14.04.2008).

[88] Stephan De Spiegeleire, “Of Buffers and Bridges. Some Geodetic Thoughts on European Stability in the Post-Cold War Era,” 13 January 1994, http://ourworld.compuserve.com/home pages/sdspieg/buffer.htm (accessed 14.04.2008).

[89] George Kennan, “The Future of Soviet Communism,” *The New Leader* (18 June, 1956): 6, quoted in: Edward Chaszar, “The Possibility of a Neutralized Zone in Central Europe,” in *Toward a New Central Europe, A Symposium on the Problems of the Danubian Nations,* ed. Francis Wagner (Astor Park: Danubian Press, 1970), http://www.hungarian-history.hu/lib/wagner/wagner04.htm (accessed 14.04.2008).

they are hostile,"[90] and as one of the Founding Fathers of the United States Alexander Hamilton affirmed: "It has... become a sort of axiom in politics that vicinity, or nearness of situation, constitutes nations' natural enemies."[91] Bordering countries interact more with each other and, hence, have more grounds for conflict, while countries that are not in each other's vicinity have less capabilities and willingness to wage war against each other (as transporting armies and military equipment over long distances is very costly). Thus, the contiguity of rival great powers negatively affects stability in the international system. States often adopt a forward defense strategy, positioning their armed forces near their frontiers, which increases the risk of border incidents between their troops standing face-to-face and often triggers a full-scale war.[92] An interesting research carried out by British mathematician Lewis Richardson revealed that in about 180 wars from 1820 to 1945, the vast majority of belligerent parties shared a common border, while only in 12 cases (6.7%) they were not contiguous.[93] Several other studies discovered that the number of frontiers a country has positively correlates to that country's participation in wars.

Stephan De Spiegeleire supposes that systemic stability is enhanced when rival states are kept apart by a buffer since a potential attacker (assumed to be a rational and unitary actor) makes calculations on the expected utility of waging a war, and the existing buffer adds to the list of his military expenditures. So, the buffer – whether a buffer state or a buffer zone – stabilizes the relationship between rival powers for two main reasons:

- A potential aggressor takes into account the military capabilities of the buffer. Even though the buffer may not have sufficient strength to repel the attack by itself, the aggressor knows that prior to reaching the territory of its rival it needs to defeat the buffer's armed forces;

---

[90] Martin Wight, *Power Politics,* ed. Hedley Bull and Carsten Holbraad (London: Leicester University Press, Royal Institute of International Affairs, 1995), 157.

[91] Alexander Hamilton, *The Federalist,* No. 5, 33, quoted in: Martin Wight, *Power Politics,* ed. Hedley Bull and Carsten Holbraad (London: Leicester University Press, Royal Institute of International Affairs, 1995), 157, 158.

[92] Stephan De Spiegeleire, "Of Buffers and Bridges. Some Geodetic Thoughts on European Stability in the Post-Cold War Era," 13 January 1994, http://ourworld.compuserve.com/homepages/sdspieg/buffer.htm (accessed 16.04.2008).

[93] Lewis Richardson, *Arms and Insecurity. A Mathematical Study of the Causes and Origins of War, and Statistics of Deadly Quarrels* (Pittsburgh: Boxwood Press, 1960), quoted in: Stephan De Spiegeleire, "Of Buffers and Bridges. Some Geodetic Thoughts on European Stability in the Post-Cold War Era," 13 January 1994, http://ourworld.compuserve.com/homepages/sdspieg/buffer.htm (accessed 16.04.2008).

- A potential aggressor envisages the possibility of an alliance between its rival power and the buffer, which may be formed in order to balance and deter the aggressor. However, the buffer may tilt the balance between the buffered powers only when their military potentials are closely equal.[94]

Of course, the buffer state cannot defeat either of the great powers, but it can hold up an invasion and give additional time to another power to mobilize its resources and draw up a plan of retaliatory actions.[95] Anyway, a potential aggressor has to take into account the buffer factor. De Spiegeleire believes that rational buffered actors will be interested in keeping the buffer between them, since the necessity to cross the buffer's territory as a prerequisite to the possible victory over a rival gives both powers the chance of transferring the hostilities to the buffer zone and thereby saving their territories from devastation. Each buffered power actually undermines its own security by engaging in territorial aggrandizement at the expense of the buffer, destroying what may have been an effective protective barrier. Thus, the buffer phenomenon has a dual positive effect on the macro stability of the international system: first, it minimizes threats emanating from the contiguity of rival powers, and second, it adds its inner stabilizing effect to the system.[96]

Buffer zones are particularly useful in preventing border skirmishes between enemy forces. In the opinion of Thomas Ross, had there been such a zone between Iran and Iraq, they might have avoided the war in 1980.[97]

In the modern world, buffer states can greatly contribute to the rapprochement and reconciliation of historical adversaries by serving as an economic and political bridge between them. One of the best examples of such practice is

---

[94] Stephan De Spiegeleire, "Of Buffers and Bridges. Some Geodetic Thoughts on European Stability in the Post-Cold War Era," 13 January 1994, http://ourworld.compuserve.com/homepages/sdspieg/buffer.htm (accessed 16.04.2008).

[95] Nicholas Spykman, "Frontiers, Security and International Organization," *Geographical Review,* Vol. 32, No. 3 (1942): 440.

[96] Stephan De Spiegeleire, "Of Buffers and Bridges. Some Geodetic Thoughts on European Stability in the Post-Cold War Era," 13 January 1994, http://ourworld.compuserve.com/homepages/sdspieg/buffer.htm (accessed 16.04.2008). De Spiegeleire distinguishes between micro and macro stability of the international system. Macro stability means the stability of the basic contours of global or regional geostrategic configuration, while micro-stability refers to the stability of certain limited areas of the international system and its elements. For instance, the Cold War system was unstable on the macro level and relatively stable on the micro level (i.e. stable within the power poles). However, after that we are witnessing a reverse picture: on the micro level there are numerous ethnic and religious conflicts in different regions of the world, whereas the on the macro level the international system has remained stable so far.

Uruguay, which, since its formation in 1828 as a buffer between Brazil and Argentina, has not only helped to bring stability to Southern Latin America, but became a genuine bridge linking these two countries (as a trade corridor, international tourist zone, and so forth);[98] In the 21st century, the countries of the Baltic region and the South Caucasus have the potential of performing the same function between Russia and the West. However, as Alexander Rondeli remarks, in order for that to happen, geoeconomics must completely replace geopolitics, if this is possible at all.[99]

From a historical perspective, it appears that many great powers have recognized the positive influence of the buffer/vacuum effect. For example, the Greek city-states surrounded themselves with man-made waste zones, and the Romans followed suit by destroying twenty-three cities in Latium for this purpose;[100] In the second half of the 19th century, when the borders of the Russian Empire in Central Asia came close to those of the British-controlled India, the two powers deemed it appropriate to separate their possessions by a belt of buffer states such as Tibet, Afghanistan and Persia, which were left independent and untouched for a relatively long time, and in 1895 they even created a narrow Wakhan Corridor (a strip of land now connecting Afghanistan with China) in order to avoid direct territorial contact between each other; In 1815, the European Great Powers agreed on the buffer status for Switzerland and the Netherlands, in 1831 and in 1839 – for Belgium, and in 1867 – for Luxembourg, etc. Nonetheless, one may also notice that in most cases the driving force behind such decisions was something other than the apprehension by the great powers of the *magical* buffer effect.

Nicholas Spykman concludes that "buffer states have endured not merely because of the recognition of their positive protective value, but also because it has always seemed better to a nation to have the territory beyond its border in the hands of a small state than to have it become an integral part of a large military unit."[101] In the opinion of Robert Rothstein: "Various Small Powers have occasionally found their independence guaranteed because their powerful

---

97 Thomas Ross, "Buffer States: A Geographer's Perspective," in *Buffer States in World Politics,* ed. John Chay and Thomas Ross (Boulder: Westview Press, 1986), 25.

98 Joseph Tulchin, "Uruguay: The Quintessential Buffer State," in *Buffer States in World Politics,* ed. John Chay and Thomas Ross (Boulder: Westview Press, 1986), 213-229.

99 Alexander Rondeli, *The Small State in the International System* (Tbilisi: Georgian Foundation for Strategic and International Studies, Metsniereba, 2003), 170 (In Georgian language).

100 Nicholas Spykman and Abbie Rollins, "Geographic Objectives in Foreign Policy, I," *The American Political Science Review,* Vol. 33, No. 3 (1939): 397.

101 Nicholas Spykman, "Frontiers, Security and International Organization," *Geographical Review,* Vol. 32, No. 3 (1942): 441-442.

neighbors were unable to agree on any other solution,"[102] that is on neither partitioning nor relinquishing their territories. Rothstein illustrates this situation with the case of Belgium in 1831 and 1839. Probably, the same can be said about Switzerland and the Netherlands in 1815, Luxembourg in 1867 and Afghanistan in the 1870s. For example, in 1866, French Emperor Napoleon III attempted to acquire Luxembourg from the Dutch King William III, but encountered a strong resistance by the German Chancellor Otto von Bismarck. Eventually, in 1867 the Treaty of London established Luxembourg as a state with neutral status; In 1839, the British started the First Anglo-Afghan War, aiming to shift the borders of their empire farther to the north-west, and if it were not for Russia's expansion in Central Asia, Afghanistan would have probably become part of the British domain, like India, and not a buffer between the two empires (in that case, other Central Asian territories might have served as buffers between Great Britain and Russia, e.g. the Khanates of Bukhara, Khiva and Kokand).[103]

Remarkably, when the opposing great powers possess more or less equal strength, the territory between them is less likely to pass into the hands of either of them or to be divided into their spheres of influence. Great powers settle on using a certain territory as a buffer when there is a regional *balance of power* between them. As A. J. P Taylor explains, "the mutual jealousy of the Great Powers has preserved even the small states, which could not have preserved themselves."[104] Nicholas Spykman brilliantly expresses the same idea: "A small state is a vacuum in a high pressure area. It does not live because of its strength but because nobody wants its territory, or because its preservation as a buffer state or as a weight in the balance of power is of interest to a stronger nation. When the balance disappears, the small state usually disappears with it."[105] A renowned German political scholar Max Weber has also made a relevant comment: "...Switzerland is not very strongly desired as an object for incorporation. Mutual jealousies existing among neighboring communities of equal strength protect it from this fate."[106]

---

[102] Robert Rothstein, *Alliances and Small Powers* (New York: Columbia University Press, 1968), 193.

[103] David Jenkins, "The History of Afghanistan as a Buffer State," in *Buffer States in World Politics,* ed. John Chay and Thomas Ross (Boulder: Westview Press, 1986), 186.

[104] A. J. P. Taylor, *The Struggle for Mastery in Europe, 1848-1918* (Oxford: Clarendon Press, 1965), xix, quoted in: Michael Handel, Weak States in the International System (London: Frank Cass, Second Edition, 1990), 175.

[105] Nicholas Spykman, *America's Strategy in World Politics* (New York: Harcourt, Brace, 1942), 20.

[106] Max Weber, *Economy and Society,* Vol. 2, ed. Guenther Roth and Claus Wittich (New York: Bedminster Press, 1968), 910, quoted in: Michael Handel, *Weak States in the International System* (London: Frank Cass, Second Edition, 1990), 176.

Michael Partem suggests that when rival powers agree on the neutrality, i.e. buffer status of the territory between them, this shows a stalemate in their relations. When conditions change, one of the powers is likely to violate the buffer's neutrality. If a potential or existing buffer falls under the influence of either of the buffered actors, the balance of power in the system proves to be shifting in favour of that particular power.[107] Thus, the buffer state becomes a target of great power expansion in the event of the buffer system's weakening or demise. For example, when the Soviet army marched into Afghanistan in 1979, the buffer function of this country was insignificant for several reasons. After India gained independence in 1947, Great Britain withdrew from Central Asia, and Afghanistan remained as a buffer between the USSR and the U.S. sphere of influence, which included Pakistan and Iran. However, both Pakistan and Iran were not themselves strong enough to balance the Soviet Union, while the United States was too far away and unwilling at that moment to fully counter the Soviet influence in the region. Moreover, following the Islamic Revolution of 1979, Iran repudiated the status of a U.S. ally. The outcome of this situation for Afghanistan, in the phrase of an American scholar David Jenkins, may be compared to that of "...two vacuum cleaners applying equal suction upon a ping-pong ball. When one vacuum cleaner is removed, the ball is sucked into the other."[108] One can use the same analogy in regard to the potential buffer states of Central Asia and the South Caucasus in the 1990s, when after the collapse of the Soviet Union, they were instantly pulled towards the U.S. sphere of influence.

Although, the existence of buffer states is largely conditioned by the will of great powers and regional balances of power, buffer states may also emerge as a result of the decline or the fall of an empire or under a regional *balance of weakness*.[109] Martin Wight remarks that each dominant power at its zenith has absorbed neighboring buffer states, but if the dominant power happened to be defeated, the buffer states re-established their independence.[110] However, such "occasional" or "seasonal" buffers are, as a rule, very short-lived, since they either fall into the hands of another power or ultimately return to the realm of their former patron. For example, during its long history Korea enjoyed self-rule only

---

107 Michael Partem, "The Buffer System in International Relations," *Journal of Conflict Resolution*, Vol. 27, No. 1 (1983): 18.

108 David Jenkins, "The History of Afghanistan as a Buffer State," in *Buffer States in World Politics*, ed. John Chay and Thomas Ross (Boulder: Westview Press, 1986), 187.

109 Michael Handel, *Weak States in the International System* (London: Frank Cass, Second Edition, 1990), 180; Robert Rothstein, Alliances and Small Powers (New York: Columbia University Press, 1968), 194.

in periods when China and Japan were relatively weak and busy with their own affairs. Every time each or both of these powers grew stronger, Korea was the first object of their expansionist policies; Similarly, Georgian kingdoms mostly gathered strength and united under a single ruler when they did not face a strong external enemy. After the abolishment of the Russian Empire in 1917, Georgia, along with Armenia and Azerbaijan, declared independence, but the three republics, which existed in 1918-1921, failed to serve as effective buffers between Soviet Russia and the Ottoman Empire, just as Lithuania, Latvia, Estonia, Poland and Czechoslovakia proved to be unsuccessful barriers against the Soviet and Nazi aggressions by the end of the interwar period (1918-1939), the main reasons for that being their insufficient military strength and the lack of their powerful neighbors' consent to their existence. Though there are some exceptions to that rule as well. Due to the bravery, unity and determination shown in 1939-1940 and again in 1944, Finland managed to defend its sovereignty and, thus, preserve its buffer role through the rest of the 20th century.

Great powers try their best to prevent their rivals from annexing buffer states or converting them into their satellites. Under the balance of power (and sometimes even in its absence) any attempt by one of the buffered powers to invade the buffer, causes reciprocal actions by the other buffered power(s). Owing to that, the buffer may stay unharmed (for instance, in 1870 Germany and France did not violate Belgium's neutrality fearing British involvement), but it may also become a shatterbelt or a battleground, eventually bringing about its devastation or partitioning by the great powers into their spheres of influence. The history of Korea, Poland, Cambodia, Lebanon, Georgia and some other countries provides many examples of such a tragic experience.

Therefore, the viability of buffer states somewhat depends on their internal strength, i.e. their ability to keep the buffered actors at peace, as well as, to a larger extent, on the willingness of the great powers to sustain them as buffers.[111]

---

[110] Martin Wight, *Power Politics,* ed. Hedley Bull and Carsten Holbraad (London: Leicester University Press, Royal Institute of International Affairs, 1995), 161.

[111] Alexander Rondeli, *The Small State in the International System* (Tbilisi: Georgian Foundation for Strategic and International Studies, Metsniereba, 2003), 165 (In Georgian language).

Chapter Six

THE FOREIGN POLICIES OF BUFFER STATES

The Emir of Afghanistan Abdur Rahman Khan* once compared his country to a swan on a lake with bears on one shore and wolves on the opposite shore, ready to snatch it up should she swim too close. The foreign policy mission of buffer states is to swim safely in such a lake. Both the proposed metaphor and reality demonstrate how difficult that task actually is, especially in light of the fact that buffers are weak states and great powers determine their fate: either by sanctioning their neutrality, agreeing on their partition or using their territory as an avenue for war against each other.[112]

The fate of buffer states is not the one to be envied. Small/weak states located on the periphery of the international system feel much more secure than those that are caught up in the middle of great power games.[113] Preserving sovereignty is a perennial issue for buffer states. The buffer may at any time become the first victim of a war between its more powerful neighbors and, thus, it generally wishes for a friendlier environment and pursues a cautious, less provocative foreign policy.

The success of the buffer state's foreign policy can roughly be determined by the following two criteria: 1) the persistence over time of its buffer status, and 2) the eventual subduing of conflict between the buffered powers.[114]

---

* The ruler of Afghanistan in 1880-1901.

112 Michael Partem, "The Buffer System in International Relations," *Journal of Conflict Resolution,* Vol. 27, No. 1 (1983): 19.

113 Michael Handel, *Weak States in the International System* (London: Frank Cass, Second Edition, 1990), 180; Robert Rothstein, *Alliances and Small Powers* (New York: Columbia University Press, 1968), 72.

114 Olav Knudsen, "Eastern Europe: The Buffer Effect of a Cordon Sanitaire," in *Buffer States in World Politics,* ed. John Chay and Thomas Ross (Boulder: Westview Press, 1986), 90.

In the opinion of Michael Partem, there are three main types of foreign policy that the buffer state may pursue:

1. Neutrality;
2. Leaning to one of the buffered powers; and
3. Relying on a third power.[115]

I would add that the first and the third choices help the buffer state to maintain its buffer status, while the second strategy turns it into the quasi-buffer state.

Neutrality, first of all, means that the buffer state is non-aligned in the conflict between its neighboring great powers and does not permit either of them to deploy armed forces on its soil. In most cases, great powers impose neutrality upon small/weak states. For example, Switzerland was neutralized in 1815, Belgium – in 1831, Luxembourg – in 1867, Cambodia – in 1954, Laos – in 1962, and so forth. The buffer state need not have a neutral status under the international law, i.e. its neutrality does not have to be declared by an international agreement or some unilateral legal act (just as Sweden's neutrality is not based on any document). However, in many instances buffer states do live under legally binding permanent neutrality (e.g. Switzerland, Austria, Cambodia, Georgia in 1918-1921, etc).

Robert Rothstein emphasizes that the policies of neutrality and non-alignment have always appealed to small powers, but the possibility of withdrawing from great power struggles and enjoying periods of peace devoted to internal development is the eternal myth for most small states, since their neutrality is viable only under a relative equilibrium of power in the international system.[116] When the balance breaks down, the buffer state is no longer willing or able to defend its neutrality, whereas as soon as the balance is re-established, it tries or is forced to revert to the non-aligned position. For example, in 1920 Belgium formed a military alliance with France, which ended its long-time neutrality. However, when Great Britain, Italy and Germany also became the guarantors of its borders under the Locarno Treaties of 1925 (in addition to France), and as the subsequent resurgence of Germany had more or less restored the balance of power in Europe, Belgium felt the need to denounce its military accord with France and eventually did so in 1936. Yet, its new promise to prevent any foreign country

---

[115] Michael Partem, "The Buffer System in International Relations," *Journal of Conflict Resolution,* Vol. 27, No. 1 (1983): 20.

[116] Robert Rothstein, *Alliances and Small Powers* (New York: Columbia University Press, 1968), 30-31.

from using its territory as a corridor or a military base for attacking other countries was broken in 1940, as Belgium proved to be defenseless against Nazi Germany;[117] Similarly, the demise of British and French influence in the Middle East following the Suez Crisis of 1956 finally undermined Lebanon's neutrality.[118]

In order to maintain its buffer status, the weak state in question must convince the great powers that its neutrality serves their interests. In the opinion of a Lebanese scholar Joseph Maila, the government of the buffer state will assert its neutrality and non-alignment in all circumstances, but may not dispel the doubts of its greater neighbours, which see it as a permanent source of problems.[119] According to Annette Baker Fox, the neutrality of small states may even take the forms of neutral alliance and unneutral neutrality,[120] which provides great powers with additional reasons for assaulting them. For example, after the Six Day War of 1967 and the October War of 1973, a large number of Palestinian refugees arrived in Lebanon, leading, over time, to the establishment of military bases of the Palestinian Liberation Organization and the deployment of Syrian troops on Lebanese territory. Thus, Lebanon's neutrality became a fiction, and in 1982 Israel responded to the Syrian military moves by launching the invasion of southern Lebanon.[121]

Robert Rothstein holds that the policy of neutrality is dangerous for small powers, which find themselves within the realm of great power interests and activity.[122] Great powers often perceive the neutrality of their small neighbors as a threat. For instance, in 1939 Viacheslav Molotov, People's Commissar for Foreign Affairs of the Soviet Union, declared: "We cannot permit small states to be used against the USSR. Neutral Baltic states – that is too insecure;"[123] In 1956, the Soviet Union brutally crushed Hungary's attempt to leave the Warsaw Pact and

---

117 Ibid., 82-115.

118 Robert McColl, "The Geopolitical Demise of Lebanon: Consequences of a Political and Military Buffer," in *Buffer States in World Politics,* ed. John Chay and Thomas Ross (Boulder: Westview Press, 1986), 140.

119 Joseph Maila, "Buffer States: The Issue of Sovereignty," in *Buffer States in World Politics,* ed. John Chay and Thomas Ross (Boulder: Westview Press, 1986), 38-39.

120 See: Annette Baker Fox, *The Power of Small States: Diplomacy in World War II* (Chicago: The University of Chicago Press, 1959).

121 Robert McColl, "The Geopolitical Demise of Lebanon: Consequences of a Political and Military Buffer," in *Buffer States in World Politics,* ed. John Chay and Thomas Ross (Boulder: Westview Press, 1986), 143-152.

122 Robert Rothstein, *Alliances and Small Powers* (New York: Columbia University Press, 1968), 34.

assume a neutral status. The Soviet attitude was later expressed by Imre Horvath, the Foreign Minister of the restored Communist regime in Hungary, who said: "We approve of the neutrality of certain capitalist countries since it [...] means standing apart from the conquerors and those ready to go to war, [while] the neutrality of a Socialist country represents an underhanded attack on the cause of peace and Socialism and its betrayal."[124]

Therefore, the policy of neutrality cannot solve all the problems faced by buffer states nor can it guarantee their survival. Sometimes an alliance with one of the great powers is far more expedient for small states than their attempts to preserve neutrality. For example, as Robert Rothstein remarks, Belgium chose to denounce its military accord with France just when it began to appear advantageous and the danger, which it was designed to combat, actually arose.[125]

A great Florentine philosopher Niccolo Machiavelli advises a prince that in case of a conflict between his two powerful neighbors, he, without any reservation, should declare himself in favour of one party against the other, which is more beneficial than standing neutral, since after the war is over, he will invariably fall prey to the conqueror. Whereas when a prince declares himself in favour of one side, if his ally wins, he has more chances to survive and prosper as the victor is indebted to him, while if his ally loses, the latter may still offer him some assistance. Besides, the vanquished power can rise again in the near future. Although, Machiavelli also says that a prince must never make an alliance with someone more powerful than himself for the purpose of attacking others (since after the war he will be at the discretion of the winner), he adds that a prince can use such tactics if the necessity to survive compells him to do so.[126]

When the buffer state enters into a military alliance with either of the buffered powers, it becomes the quasi-buffer state, which may invite the armed forces of the power which it buffers on its territory. This is less likely to happen on the buffer's own initiative. In most cases, one of the buffered powers (usually the one

---

123 Alber Tarulis, *Soviet Policy Towards the Baltic States, 1918-1940* (South Bend: University of Notre Dame Press, 1959), 154, 155, quoted in: Michael Handel, *Weak States in the International System* (London: Frank Cass, Second Edition, 1990), 72.

124 Edward Chaszar, "The Possibility of a Neutralized Zone in Central Europe," in *Toward a New Central Europe, A Symposium on the Problems of the Danubian Nations,* ed. Francis Wagner (Astor Park: Danubian Press, 1970), http://www.hungarian-history.hu/lib/wagner/wagner04.htm (accessed 20.04.2008).

125 Robert Rothstein, *Alliances and Small Powers* (New York: Columbia University Press, 1968), 115.

126 Nicolo Machiavelli, *The Prince,* trans. W. K. Marriott (The Project Gutenberg E-Book no. 1232, 11.02.2006), http://www.gutenberg.org/files/1232/1232.txt (accessed 27.04.2008).

which is stronger at the moment) imposes an unequal – "wolf and sheep,"[127] "cat and mouse"[128] or "Al Capone"[129] – alliance on the buffer.

Michael Partem believes that pressures on the buffer state to lean on one side intensify in three situations, when:

1. The rivalry between the buffered powers heats up;
2. The level of capabilities shifts dramatically to the advantage of one of the buffered powers; or
3. Internal dissension (civil war, separatism, terrorism, etc.) threatens domestic upheaval in the buffer state.[130]

Usually if a state is faced with threats to its sovereignty from another state, it can do three things: 1) defend itself by its own strength, 2) ally with another power, that is balance the aggressor, or 3) ally with the source of the threat, that is bandwagon.[131] Michael Handel thinks that most weak states side with the stronger and more threatening power [i.e. often bandwagon] and switch their position when the balance of power in the system changes, deserting the declining original ally and joining the ascending power that still needs help.[132] Annette Baker Fox refers to such behavior as "anti-balance of power."[133] Historically, buffer states have often resorted to such tactics in order to survive. For example, in 1940 Hungary, Romania and Bulgaria openly declared their support for the Berlin-Rome-Tokyo axis, etc.

Joseph Maila argues that the foreign policy orientation of the buffer state depends greatly on the level of its sovereignty. When the buffer state's territorial integrity is breached, it will try to conclude a military alliance with the stronger

---

127 Robert Rothstein, *Alliances and Small Powers* (New York: Columbia University Press, 1968), 117.

128 Michael Handel, *Weak States in the International System* (London: Frank Cass, Second Edition, 1990), 72.

129 Robert Keohane, "Lilliputians' Dilemmas: Small States in International Politics," *International Organization,* Vol. 23, No. 2 (1969): 302. In the 1920s, Chicago businessmen paid money to Al Capone, protecting themselves not only from other mafia gangs, but mainly from Al Capone's own thugs.

130 Michael Partem, "The Buffer System in International Relations," *Journal of Conflict Resolution,* Vol. 27, No. 1 (1983): 21.

131 Alexander Rondeli, *International Relations* (Tbilisi: Neker, Third Edition, 2006), 156. See also: Stephen Walt, *The Origins of Alliances* (Ithaca: Cornell University Press, 1990).

132 Michael Handel, *Weak States in the International System* (London: Frank Cass, Second Edition, 1990), 186.

133 Annette Baker Fox, *The Power of Small States: Diplomacy in World War II* (Chicago: The University of Chicago Press, 1959), 187.

power and restore its territorial integrity with its help. While if the buffer state's territorial integrity is guaranteed by the great powers, it will prefer to preserve its neutrality and buffer status. If the buffer state has a challenged sovereignty and it neither forms an alliance nor manages to restore its territorial integrity by other means, its foreign policy could be considered as a complete failure, which usually happens to very weak buffer states sinking into disintegration because of civil strife or other detrimental domestic political processes (such are the cases of Lebanon in 1970-1980, Cambodia in 1970s, and so on).[134]

When the stability of the international system is under threat, opposing great powers tend to be more interested in expanding the circle of their allies rather than maintaining buffer states. Under such circumstances, the independence of buffer states runs counter to the interests of their stronger neighbors, eventually causing their devastation by wars and/or drawing into compulsory alliances with great powers (the history of Georgia, Belgium, Poland and other countries contains plenty of such moments).

The government of the buffer state knows that its leaning to one side will cause a harsh reaction from the other side and, hence, the only thing it may often consider worthwhile is to engage in diplomatic maneuvering. For instance, in the 1950s, Afghanistan refused to join the Central Treaty Organization (CENTO) as it feared irritating the Soviet Union. However, for some years it received military aid from both the USSR and the United States; In 1948 Finland signed the Treaty of Friendship, Cooperation and Mutual Assistance with the Soviet Union, assuming the obligation to refrain from membership in any alliance or coalition directed against the Soviet Union.[135]

When the buffer state finds it hard to remain neutral under the cross-cutting pressure from the buffered powers, especially if aligning with one of them may result in a war with the other and even in losing its independence, the buffer is left with an additional option – an alliance with a third power, which owing to the fact that it does not border the buffer directly, might be less interested in dominating it and more concerned with preventing the expansion of its two rivals by deterring their designs on the buffer. The third power strategy is sometimes the most effective one for buffer states. For example, in 1828, due to the British diplomatic intervention, Uruguay managed to avoid the dilemma of choosing sides in the war between Brazil and Argentina, as both parties recognized its independence. Since then Uruguay has many times successfully appealed for support to Great Britain

[134] Joseph Maila, "Buffer States: The Issue of Sovereignty," in *Buffer States in World Politics,* ed. John Chay and Thomas Ross (Boulder: Westview Press, 1986), 36-37.

and the United States. However, relying on a third power usually brings short-term policy gains only. For instance, in 1958, in order to halt the aggression of Syria and Egypt, Lebanon asked the United States for assistance and managed to defend its sovereignty after U.S. troops landed on its territory, but later, in the 1970s, Lebanon failed to repeat its successful move and obtain the same degree of external support; In May 1918, the young Democratic Republic of Georgia, in order to neutralize the Turkish threat to its independence, invited German troops on its soil and in November 1918, after Germany surrendered in the First World War, replaced them with the British armed forces. However, as the latter left Georgia in May 1920, the newly established republic found itself unprotected from the Turkish and Russian expansions and ceased to exist in February 1921, after it was occupied by the Soviet army, etc.

Michael Handel and Robert Rothstein also believe that choosing a distant great power as an ally is not a reliable strategy for small/weak states, since the commitment of a remote great power to come to the aid of a small power in case it is attacked by its more powerful neighbor, may be less certain. As an example, because of its great distance from Central America, it was difficult for the Soviet Union to provide help to Cuba during the Cold War.[136] This argument may be further strengthened by several facts from Georgia's history. In 1587, King Alexander II of Kakheti, in order to defend his land from the Persian and Ottoman encroachments, signed the "Book of Pledge" with a third power – Russia. However, in 1605 this did not save him and his kingdom from the fury of Shah Abbas the Great of Persia. In 1722, King Vakhtang VI of Kartli, in an effort to counter both the Persian and Ottoman threats, established contacts with Russia, but waited in vain (together with his army) near Ganja for military assistance from the Russian Emperor Peter I the Great, which resulted in the ravaging of his country and his expulsion shortly afterwards, etc.

States within the buffer zone may theoretically form an alliance among themselves – a buffer coalition. For instance, in 1919 many Western statesmen hoped that few small Eastern European states would form some kind of a federation, which could have greatly enhanced the buffer effect of this region.

---

135 Timo Vihavainen, "After the War: Finland's Relations with the Soviet Union, 1944-1991," November 2001, http://virtual.finland.fi/finfo/english/after.html (accessed 29.04.2008).

136 Michael Handel, *Weak States in the International System* (London: Frank Cass, Second Edition, 1990), 128; Robert Rothstein, *Alliances and Small Powers* (New York: Columbia University Press, 1968), 118.

However, despite certain indications, this scenario did not materialize.[137] In 1921, Czechoslovakia, Yugoslavia and Romania established Little Entente in order to thwart possible Hungarian revisionism and diminish great power influence in their region, but in 1938, when Yugoslavia and Romania left Czechoslovakia alone in the face of the German threat, the alliance broke down.[138]

As Robert Rothstein points out, alliances composed solely of small powers are worthless as their combined strength cannot match with that of the great powers.[139] Likewise, Annette Baker Fox concludes that small power alliances are ineffective since the sum of their power is weakness.[140]

Thus, the foreign policy orientation of the buffer state is ultimately of no critical importance as its fate is to an immense extent determined by the balance of power in the international system and the will of the buffered powers. When the power equilibrium in the system is upset, the buffer state may either lose its buffer status or stop to exist at all.

---

137 Stephan De Spiegeleire, "Of Buffers and Bridges. Some Geodetic Thoughts on European Stability in the Post-Cold War Era," 13 January, 1994: 8, 18, http://ourworld.compuserve.com/homepages/sdspieg/buffer.htm (accessed 04.05.2008).

138 Robert Rothstein, *Alliances and Small Powers* (New York: Columbia University Press, 1968), 128-177.

139 Ibid., 117.

140 Annette Baker Fox, *The Power of Small States: Diplomacy in World War II* (Chicago: The University of Chicago Press, 1959), 185.

Chapter Seven

THE BUFFER SYSTEM

The buffer and the buffered powers make up the buffer system, which consists of at least three elements: one buffer state and two rival great powers (*see diagram 1*). In fact, the number of the buffered powers can be more than two. For example, before its tripartite division in the 18th century, Poland served as a buffer between Russia, Prussia and Austria. The buffered powers in the buffer system may also be either alliances composed of several great powers or their spheres of influence, i.e. great powers joined by their weaker allies, while the buffer itself may as well be represented by a number of small/weak states, i.e. the buffer zone. For example, the European neutral states [Switzerland, Austria, Sweden, Finland] were buffers between the Warsaw Pact and the North Atlantic Alliance.[141]

According to Olav Knudsen, the conditions for the existence of the buffer system include:

1. The buffer's geographical location between opposing greater powers;
2. A rough power parity between these rival great powers; and
3. A substantial power disparity between the great and small powers involved.[142]

Michael Partem identifies the following characteristics of the buffer system:

---

141 Stephan De Spiegeleire, "Of Buffers and Bridges. Some Geodetic Thoughts on European Stability in the Post-Cold War Era," 13 January, 1994: 8, http://ourworld.compuserve.com/homepages/sdspieg/buffer.htm (accessed 07.05.2008).

142 Olav Knudsen, "Eastern Europe: The Buffer Effect of a Cordon Sanitaire," in *Buffer States in World Politics,* ed. John Chay and Thomas Ross (Boulder: Westview Press, 1986), 90.

- B (buffer) is contiguous with A and C (buffered powers);
- A and C both perceive their probability of defeating B in a bilateral conflict as greater than 50%;
- A and C have more or less the same capabilities;
- B is not able to determine the outcome of conflict between A and C;
- B tries to avoid a military alliance with both A and C.

The crucial determinant of the buffer system is the conflict (rivalry and struggle for dominance) between the buffered powers. Moreover, this has to be a true high-intensity power competition. For example, Belgium, the Netherlands and Luxembourg cannot be thought of as buffers today, because the conflict between Germany, France and Great Britain had ceased after 1945.[143]

If at least one of the elements of the buffer system disappears or alters significantly, the system will halt functioning. This, in turn, can happen if:

1. One of the buffered powers eliminates the other;
2. The buffered powers become friends/allies;
3. One of the buffered powers coerces the buffer into an alliance or subjugates it;
4. The buffer's capabilities equates with those of either of the buffered powers.

In the first case, the buffer system is transformed into the unipolar/hierarchical regional system, in the second case – the alliance system, in the third case – the quasi-buffer system and in the fourth case – the multipolar/three-polar system.

Some buffer states have retained their buffer role despite numerous changes of actors in their regional buffer system. For instance, Cambodia was a buffer, and at times a quasi-buffer, from the 15th through the 19th centuries between the Thai and Vietnam Empires and afterwards, in the 20th century, was interposed between North Vietnam and South Vietnam, i.e. the Communist and Western spheres of influence;[144] In 1945, Korea, as a traditional buffer/quasi-buffer between China and Japan, witnessed one of its buffered powers being replaced by the U.S. sphere of influence (later, the U.S.-Japan alliance).

Michael Partem assumes that the buffer system operates according to the rational calculations of the buffered powers (Partem based this hypothesis on the

---

[143] Michael Partem, "The Buffer System in International Relations," *Journal of Conflict Resolution*, Vol. 27, No. 1 (1983): 13, 16.

rational unitary actor model formulated by a well-known American scholar Bruce Bueno de Mesquita).[145] Partem suggests that each buffered power makes cost-benefit calculations before going to war with the other and decides to attack its rival only when it considers the expected utility of such an action to exceed its likely costs. In this situation, the buffer factor increases war expenses for both buffered powers and, thus, contributes to preserving peace among them.

As noted above, in Michael Partem's model of the buffer system, each buffered power considers the probability of defeating the buffer in a bilateral conflict to be greater than 50%. Correspondingly, the buffer state judges the probability of being defeated in a bilateral conflict with either of the buffered powers as greater than 50%. If there are two buffered powers (A and C) and one buffer (B) in the system, the probability (P) will take the following form:

$$Pab > 0{,}5 \text{ and } Pcb > 0{,}5$$

where P is the probability of winning the conflict (greater than 50%) in the first case by A against B and in the second case by C against B. However, it seems impossible to pinpoint just how much greater than 50% this probability can be. Moreover, these formulas imply that A and C have more or less the same capabilities and, hence, cannot change this bipolar regional system into the unipolar one.

$$Pac - Pca \cong 0 \text{ or } Pca \cong Pac$$

This means that the probabilities of A defeating C or, vice versa, C defeating A, are identical.[146]

In my opinion, if the capabilities of the buffered powers are unequal in absolute terms, the buffer system may still function properly: this can happen when the buffer is geographically much closer to the weaker of the buffered powers than to the stronger one. For example, today Russia is definitely weaker than the United States, but the countries of the South Caucasus and Central Asia may develop into buffer states, since Russia's willingness to influence these regions and its pressure on them largely exceeds that of the United States. In this

---

144 Ibid., 5.

145 See: Bruce Bueno De Mesquita's *The War Trap* (New Haven: Yale University Press, 1981) and "Measuring Systemic Polarity," *Journal of Conflict Resolution,* Vol. 19, No. 2 (1975): 187-216.

146 Michael Partem, "The Buffer System in International Relations," *Journal of Conflict Resolution,* Vol. 27, No. 1 (1983): 7-10.

case, geographical proximity compensates for relative weakness, which can be demonstrated by the following formula:

$$PQab = \frac{Pab - Pba}{Dab}$$

where PQab – the probability of A wielding influence over B, that is of turning it into its quasi-buffer is directly proportional to the difference between the capabilities of A and B (the probability of defeating each other in a bilateral conflict) and inversely proportional to the geographical distance between them (Dab). Of course, this formula cannot fully explain the transformation of buffer systems into quasi-buffer systems simply because it does not include B's foreign policy orientation and some other factors as variables, but I think that in most cases this formula works. It describes, for example, why at certain stages of the Cold War the majority of Eastern European states were actually quasi-buffers of the Soviet Union, while Canada and several countries of Latin America served as quasi-buffers of the United States, but it fails to explain, for example, why Cuba was incorporated into the Soviet Union's sphere of influence in the 1960s, or why two countries of the South Caucasus (namely Georgia and Azerbaijan) are now attracted to the Western political and military arrangements, while the third country (Armenia) is clearly leaning towards Russia.

If the balance of power in the buffer system changes, e.g. if the buffer grows so strong that either or both of the buffered powers perceive the probability of defeating it in a bilateral conflict as less than 50% (in other words, if the third pole emerges in between the two power poles), the buffer system will cease to exist. Even though there are not many historical facts to illustrate this trend, a few examples may still be presented. In the second half of the 19th century, Prussia finally united all German lands and became one of the most powerful empires in Europe;[147] At the end of the 11th century, the Kingdom of Georgia under King David IV the Builder (1089-1125) developed into the main center of power in the region, stretching its borders "from Nikopsia to Daruband and from Ossetia to Aragats"* and later, under Queen Tamar (1184-1213), expanded its sphere of influence even further, etc.

---

147 Ibid., 7-9.

* In modern-day geographical terms, from Tuapse (Krasnodar Krai, Russia) to Derbent (Dagestan, Russia) and from North Ossetia (Russia) to Mount Aragats (Armenia).

The buffer is generally too "small" to tilt the balance of power to the advantage of either of the buffered powers by siding with it. Thus, B's ability to affect the outcome of the conflict between A and C is minimal and this can be expressed by the following equation:

$$Pabc \leq 0{,}5 \text{ and } Pcba \leq 0{,}5$$

which means that the perceived probability of each buffered power defeating its rival by adding the buffer's military potential to its own capabilities is less than 50% or, at best, equals 50%. Therefore, from a military standpoint, the buffer is an ineffective ally for the buffered powers, but it surely can be used by them as a corridor to advance against each other.[148]

Different elements of the buffer system have distinct ranges of interests, which are the following:

- A may be willing to:
  - Defeat C;
  - Control B;

- C may be willing to:
  - Defeat A;
  - Control B;

The word "control," in turn, implies that each buffered power may at different times want to:

- Annex the buffer;
- Turn the buffer into its ally/quasi-buffer; or
- Keep the buffer neutral;

- B may be willing to:
  - Stay neutral in the conflict between A and C;
  - Align with A;
  - Align with C;
  - Align with the third power (D);

---

148 Michael Partem, "The Buffer System in International Relations," *Journal of Conflict Resolution,* Vol. 27, No. 1 (1983): 10.

- D (if it exists) may be willing to prevent both A and C from enhancing their strength by subduing B.

If the buffer enters into an alliance with either of the buffered powers, the buffer system will be replaced by the quasi-buffer system, where A (or C) may be trying to deter or attack the rival C (or A) with the help of the former buffer, now its quasi-buffer (Q) (*see diagram 2*).

John Chay argues that the buffer system will survive only as long as the balances of power, interests and intentions exist between the neighboring great powers. When these conditions disappear, often leading to the subjugation of the buffer by one the powers, the buffer system will collapse.[149] Thus, the transition of the buffer system to the quasi-buffer system is caused by the disruption of the power equilibrium among the buffered powers, as well as by differences in their interests towards the buffer.

In the view of Olav Knudsen, there are several factors contributing to the preservation of the buffer system:

1. The power parity between the buffered powers. The more symmetrical (equal) the strength of the rival great powers, the less the leverage either of them can have on the buffer's foreign policy. Conversely, the more asymmetrical (unequal) the capabilities of the rivals, the more the likelihood that one of them will bring the buffer under its control and replace the buffer system with some other system. In this case, the buffer will yield to the party in conflict towards which the balance of power is shifting;
2. The equality of strategic importance (salience) of the buffer area to the buffered powers and high probability that each of them will resist attempts by the other to revise the status quo in the system. The buffer may possess natural resources, a potential military base site or some other things the contending great powers may be attracted to. Such "great power lures" could have both positive and negative consequences for the buffer, that is they can be both its assets and liabilities. If the buffer's strategic importance to the rival great powers is somewhat lop-sided, the buffer system is likely to become unstable and eventually break down, whereas if both sides show equal interest towards the buffer, the latter will be sustained and jointly exploited by the buffered powers;

149 John Chay, "Korea, a Buffer State," in *Buffer States in World Politics,* ed. John Chay and Thomas Ross (Boulder: Westview Press, 1986), 194.

3. The great costs of dominating the buffer incurred by the great powers, which, in addition to the aforementioned factors, is directly connected to the intrinsic strength of the buffer, in turn, resting on: 1) the buffer state's defense capabilities (military potential), 2) the commitment to independence within the buffer state's political elite and society, and 3) the buffer state's domestic cohesiveness – the greater the degree of internal conflict in the buffer state, the smaller its external strength on the international arena.[150]

The buffer system with non-aligned and uncontrolled states at the center and those under the influence of the great powers at the peripheries is labelled by Olav Knudsen as the buffer complex (*see diagram 3*). The buffer effect of the neutral states at the core of the buffer complex may "spill over" to the surrounding satellites. As long as the core countries actively cooperate and are supportive of each other in their relations with the great powers, they derive added protective strength, which increases their chances of staying autonomous and neutral (Northern Europe since 1948 might serve as a good illustration of such regional solidarity). The stability of the buffer complex largely depends on the success of its buffer elements in resisting pressure from the great powers. The latter are expected to try to impose their influence on the buffer area and even partition it for that purpose. If one of the buffer states in the buffer complex unilaterally concludes an alliance with one of the great powers, this will trigger disagreements among the buffer states at the core and reduce their buffer effect leading to the disruption of the buffer complex. Olav Knudsen suggests that Europe developed into a kind of a buffer complex after 1945 [probably, lasting up to 1991], but the buffer effect of its neutral, uncontrolled core – Sweden, Finland, Switzerland, Austria – was quite weak, since the opposing superpowers directly confronted each other in Europe, namely in divided Germany.[151]

---

150 Olav Knudsen, "Eastern Europe: The Buffer Effect of a Cordon Sanitaire," in *Buffer States in World Politics,* ed. John Chay and Thomas Ross (Boulder: Westview Press, 1986), 91.

151 Olav Knudsen, "Eastern Europe: The Buffer Effect of a Cordon Sanitaire," in *Buffer States in World Politics,* ed. John Chay and Thomas Ross (Boulder: Westview Press, 1986), 93-95, 107.

Conclusion

Thus, buffer states are weak, neutral states lying in a geopolitical space between rival great powers or alliances of roughly the same strength, generally established and/or maintained at the will of these power poles, geographically separating them from each other, contributing to the balance of power between them and stabilizing the international system temporarily – before the great powers choose to disturb its equilibrium. Conversely, quasi-buffer states, unlike genuine buffers, divert from the policy of neutrality either by or against their own will and serve as shields to one of the power poles, thereby acting against the balance-of-power mechanism rather than contributing to the ad hoc stability of the international system. Nevertheless, quasi-buffer states seem to have more chances of survival than buffer states – of course, if they happen to choose the "right" side in the great power confrontation. Georgia, as a potential buffer state, has apparently recognized this reality and, notwithstanding the clear and present danger from its northern neighbor Russia, is properly turning down the role of a neutral, buffer state and trying to find a place under the Western security umbrella, even that of a quasi-buffer.

The majority of buffer and quasi-buffer states have hostile physical environments and ethnically/culturally diverse populations, often coupled by the passage of important international transportation routes through their territories. Buffer and quasi-buffer states may border the contending great powers or alliances both by land and sea. Moreover, small/weak states can better perform the peacemaking buffer function if they are located an equal distance between the rival centers of power.

Great powers and alliances vie for influence over the geopolitical vacuum that might emerge between them, seeking to turn all the weak states located in this power void into their allies, agreeing to keep them as neutral buffers only in case there is a regional balance of power – that is when they fail to settle on either partitioning this geopolitical vacuum or surrendering it to one another. If the power equilibrium in the system shifts in favor of one of the poles, the buffer area is likely to become a locus of conflict, often resulting in its subjugation by the stronger, triumphant power.

Although in the long run, buffers, which are mostly small/weak states, can neither maintain the balance of power between the great powers nor deter their aggressive behavior, the stronger their armed forces and the more unified, freedom-loving their societies, the better are their chances of defending their independence and successfully performing the role of buffers. However, in order for buffer states to survive, they must, first of all, have the fortune of great powers and alliances being interested in their existence.

The buffer and quasi-buffer elements of the international system and the centers of power buffered by them can be conceived of as separate systems (or subsystems), operating under the balances between the opposing power poles' capabilities and interests towards the buffer area, as well as the buffer's intrinsic strength.

The practice of employing certain territories and countries as buffers was first introduced at a time when only regional systems of states existed and military technology was in the early stages of its development. Yet, even after the formation of the international political and economic systems covering the entire globe, the technological evolution of weapons (the invention of bomber aircraft, intercontinental ballistic missiles and nuclear weapons, to name a few), the institutionalization of the international law and the advent of the era of globalization, the buffer phenomenon as an instrument of power politics has amazingly survived into the third millennium A.D.

Nowadays the number of buffer states in the world is steadily diminishing, one of the major reasons for this being that throughout history buffer states largely failed to serve as long-term stabilizing elements of the international system. But, as long as the planet's great powers continue to struggle for influence on the international political arena and fight wars against each other, buffer states, as well as quasi-buffer states, will not disappear.

ANNEX

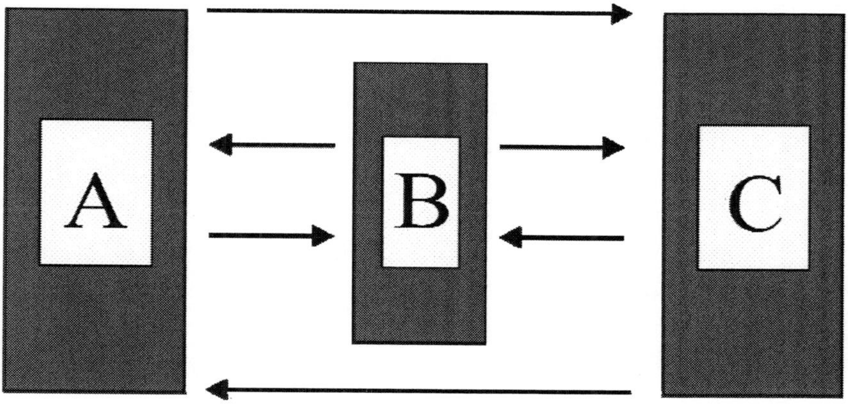

Diagram 1. The Buffer System

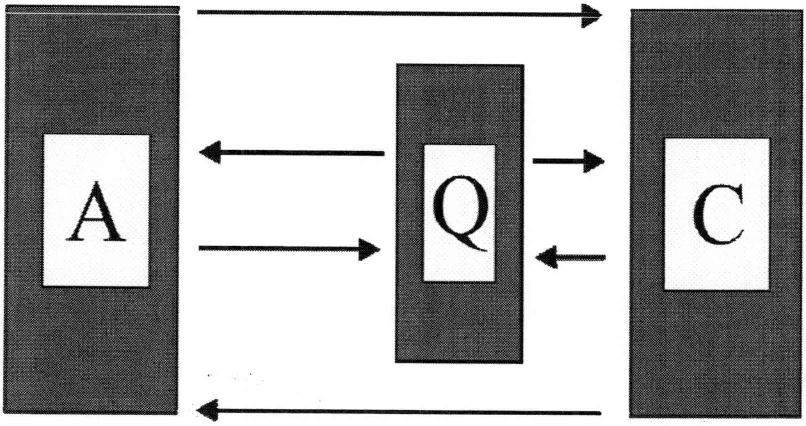

Diagram 2. The Quasi-Buffer System.

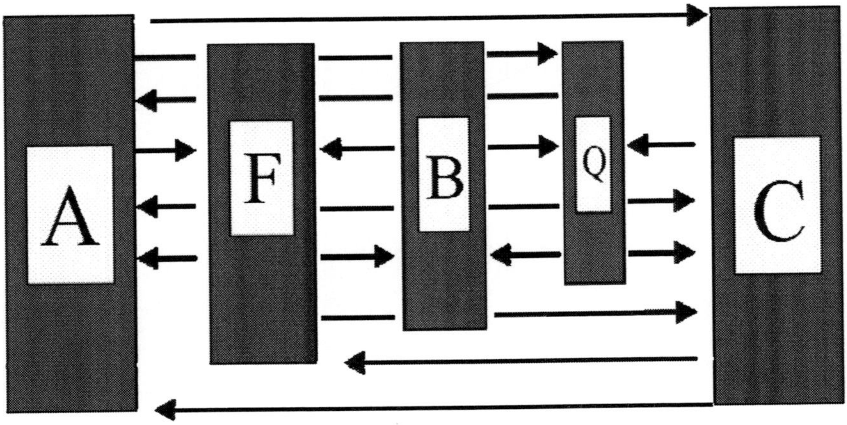

Diagram 3. The Buffer Complex.

The diagrams above show:

- A and C as buffered powers;
- B as buffer;
- Q as quasi-buffer of power C;
- F as ally/friend of power A;
- Arrows indicating foreign policy vectors of system participants.

BIBLIOGRAPHY

Brzezinski, Zbigniew. *The Grand Chessboard.* New York: Basic Books, 1997.

Baker Fox, Annette. *The Power of Small States: Diplomacy in World War II.* Chicago: The University of Chicago Press, 1959.

Bueno De Mesquita, Bruce. *The War Trap.* New Haven: Yale University Press, 1981.

Bueno De Mesquita, Bruce. "Measuring Systemic Polarity." *Journal of Conflict Resolution,* Vol. 19, No. 2 (1975): 187-216.

Chaszar, Edward. "The Possibility of a Neutralized Zone in Central Europe." In *Toward a New Central Europe, A Symposium on the Problems of the Danubian Nations,* Francis Wagner, ed. Astor Park: Danubian Press, 1970. http://www.hungarian-history.hu/lib/wagner/wagner04.htm (accessed 14.04.2008).

Chay, John and Thomas Ross, eds. *Buffer States in World Politics.* Boulder: Westview Press, 1986.

Chay, John. "Korea, a Buffer State." In *Buffer States in World Politics,* John Chay and Thomas Ross, eds., 191-211. Boulder: Westview Press, 1986.

Davitashvili, Zurab. *The Historical and Political Geography of the World.* Tbilisi: Pirveli Stamba, 2001. (In Georgian).

Debidour, Antoine. *The Diplomatic History of Europe,* Vol. I-II. Moscow: Foreign Literature Publishers, 1947 (1891). (In Russian).

De Spiegeleire, Stephan. "Of Buffers and Bridges. Some Geodetic Thoughts on European Stability in the Post-Cold War Era." 13 January 1994. http://ourworld.compuserve.com /homepages/sdspieg/buffer.htm (accessed 07.05.2008).

Encarta World English Dictionary. Microsoft Corporation, North American Edition, 2006. http://encarta.msn.com/dictionary_1861694156/buffer_state.html, http://encarta.msn.com/dictionary_1861694158/buffer_zone.html (accessed 21.01.2008).

Fazal, Tanisha. "State Death in the International System." *International Organization,* Vol. 58, No. 2 (2004): 311-344.

Gegeshidze, Archil. *Geopolitics.* Tbilisi: ESM, 1997. (In Georgian).

Handel, Michael. *Weak States in the International System.* London: Frank Cass, Second Edition, 1990 (1981).

Huntington, Samuel. "The Clash of Civilizations?" *Foreign Affairs,* Vol. 72, No. 3 (1993): 22-49. http://www.alamut.com/subj/economics/misc/clash.html (accessed 25.01.2008).

Ingalls, Gerald. "Buffer States: Outlining and Expanding Existing Theory." In *Buffer States in World Politics,* John Chay and Thomas Ross, eds., 231-240. Boulder: Westview Press, 1986.

International Relations Theory: A Chrestomathy, Tornike Turmanidze, Erekle Urushadze and Levan Duchidze, compilers, eds. Tbilisi: ICI, 2004. (In Georgian).

Jenkins, David. "The History of Afghanistan as a Buffer State." In *Buffer States in World Politics,* John Chay and Thomas Ross, eds., 171-189. Boulder: Westview Press, 1986.

Johns, Sheridan. "Southern Africa: Buffer States without a Conventional Buffer System." In *Buffer States in World Politics,* John Chay and Thomas Ross, eds., 41-66. Boulder: Westview Press. 1986.

Kelly, Philip. "Buffer Systems of Middle America." In *Buffer States in World Politics,* John Chay and Thomas Ross, eds., 67-86. Boulder: Westview Press, 1986.

Keohane, Robert. "Lilliputians' Dilemmas: Small States in International Politics." *International Organization,* Vol. 23, No. 2 (1969): 291-310.

Knudsen, Olav. "Eastern Europe: The Buffer Effect of a Cordon Sanitaire." In *Buffer States in World Politics,* John Chay and Thomas Ross, eds., 87-110. Boulder: Westview Press, 1986.

Machiavelli, Nicolo. *The Prince,* W. K. Marriott, trans. The Project Gutenberg E-Book no. 1232, 11.02.2006. http://www.gutenberg.org/files/1232/1232.txt (accessed 27.04.2008).

Mackinder, Halford. *Democratic Ideals and Reality.* New York: Henry Holt and Company, 1919.

Maila, Joseph. "Buffer States: The Issue of Sovereignty." In *Buffer States in World Politics,* John Chay and Thomas Ross, eds., 29-40. Boulder: Westview Press, 1986.

Mathisen, Trygve. *The Functions of Small States in the Strategies of the Great Powers*. Oslo: Universitetsvorlaget, 1971.

McColl, Robert. "The Geopolitical Demise of Lebanon: Consequences of a Political and Military Buffer." In *Buffer States in World Politics,* John Chay and Thomas Ross, eds., 133-152. Boulder: Westview Press, 1986.

Merriam-Webster Online Dictionary. Merriam-Webster, Inc., 2005. http://www.m-w.com/dictionary/buffer, http://www.m-w.com/dictionary/buffer%20state (accessed 21.01.2008).

Partem, Michael. "The Buffer System in International Relations." *Journal of Conflict Resolution,* Vol. 27, No. 1 (1983): 3-26.

Potter, Pitman. "Buffer State." *Encyclopedia of Social Sciences,* No. 3-4, 1930.

Random House Unabridged Dictionary. Random House, Inc., on Infoplease, 1997. http://www.infoplease.com/ipd/A0354846.html, http://www.infoplease.com/ipd/A0354848.html (accessed 21.01.2008).

Rondeli, Alexander. *International Relations*. Tbilisi: Neker, Third Edition, 2006 (1996). (In Georgian).

Rondeli, Alexander. "Regional Security Prospects in the Caucasus." In *Crossroads and Conflict: Security and Foreign Policy in the Caucasus and Central Asia,* Gary Bertsch, Cassady Craft, Scott Jones and Michael Beck, eds., 48-54. New York and London: Routledge, 2000.

Rondeli, Alexander. *The Small State in the International System.* Tbilisi: Georgian Foundation for Strategic and International Studies, Metsniereba, 2003. (In Georgian).

Ross, Thomas. "Buffer States: A Geographer's Perspective." In *Buffer States in World Politics,* John Chay and Thomas Ross, eds., 11-28. Boulder: Westview Press, 1986.

Rothstein, Robert. *Alliances and Small Powers.* New York: Columbia University Press, 1968.

Spykman, Nicholas. *America's Strategy in World Politics.* New York: Harcourt, Brace, 1942.

Spykman, Nicholas. "Frontiers, Security, and International Organization." *Geographical Review*, Vol. 32, No. 3 (1942), 436-447.

Spykman, Nicholas and Abbie Rollins. "Geographic Objectives in Foreign Policy, I." *The American Political Science Review,* Vol. 33, No. 3 (1939), 391-410.

The American Heritage Dictionary of the English Language. Houghton Mifflin Company, Fourth Edition, 2000. http://www.bartleby.com/61/31/B0533100.html, http: //www.bartleby.com/61/31/B0533100.html (accessed 20.01.2008).

The Columbia Encyclopedia. Sixth Edition, 2001-2005. http://www.bartleby.com/65/bu/ buffer.html (accessed 20.01.2008).

The Concise Oxford Dictionary of Current English, J. Sykes, ed. Oxford: Clarendon Press, Seventh Edition, 1982.

The Dictionary of Georgian Language, Arnold Chikobava, ed. Tbilisi: Georgian Academy of Sciences, 1986. (In Georgian).

The Dictionary of Government and Politics, P. H. Collin, ed. Middlesex: Peter Collin Publishing, Second Edition, 1997.

The History of Diplomacy, Vol. I, Vladimir Potiomkin, ed. Moscow: GSEI, 1941. (In Russian).

The History of Diplomacy, Vol. II-III, Vladimir Potiomkin, ed. Moscow: GIPL, 1945. (In Russian).

The Soviet Georgian Encyclopedia, Vol. II. Tbilisi: Georgian Academy of Sciences, 1977. (In Georgian).

The 2008 World Factbook. The Central Intelligence Agency. https://www.cia.gov/library /publications/the-world-factbook (accessed 12.06.2008).

Tosches, Albert. "The Albanian Lands: Contiguity and Change in a Buffer Region." In: *Buffer States in World Politics,* John Chay and Thomas Ross, eds., 111-132. Boulder: Westview Press, 1986.

Tulchin, Joseph. "Uruguay: The Quintessential Buffer State." In *Buffer States in World Politics,* John Chay and Thomas Ross, eds., 213-229. Boulder: Westview Press, 1986.

Vandenbosch, Amry. "The Small States in International Politics and Organization." *The Journal of Politics,* Vol. 26, No. 2 (1964): 293-312.

Vihavainen, Timo. "After the War: Finland's Relations with the Soviet Union 1944-1991." November 2001. http://virtual.finland.fi/finfo/english/after.html (accessed 23.09.06).

Viotti, Paul and Mark Kauppi. *International Relations Theory. Realism, Pluralism, Globalism.* New York: Macmillan, 1987.

Walt, Stephen. *The Origins of Alliances.* Ithaca: Cornell University Press, 1990.

Waltz, Kenneth. *Man, the State and War.* New York: Columbia University Press, 1954.

Wight, Martin. *Power Politics,* Hedley Bull and Carsten Holbraad, eds., London: Leicester University Press, Royal Institute of International Affairs, 1995 (1978).

Ziring, Lawrence. "Asia's Pivotal Buffer States." In *Buffer States in World Politics,* John Chay and Thomas Ross, eds., 153-170. Boulder: Westview Press, 1986.

INDEX

C

D

E

F

G

H

I

J

K

L

M

N

O

P

U

V

W

Y

Z

Weeded
Dec 5, 2025